Changing Identities

THE NEW IMMIGRANTS SERIES

Allyn & Bacon

Series Editor, Nancy Foner, State University of New York at Purchase

Changing Identities:
Vietnamese Americans, 1975-1995

James M. Freeman

Allyn and Bacon
Boston • London • Toronto • Sydney • Tokyo • Singapore

Copyright © 1995 by Allyn and Bacon
A Division of Simon and Schuster
160 Gould Street
Needham Heights, Massachusetts 02194

ISBN: 0-205-17082-X

Printed in the United States of America

10 9 8 7 6 5 4 3 2   99 98 97

Contents

Foreword to the Series

The United States is now experiencing the largest wave of immigration in the country's history. The 1990s, it is predicted, will see more new immigrants enter the United States than in any decade in American history. New immigrants from Asia, Latin America, and the Caribbean are changing the American ethnic landscape.

Until recently, immigration was associated in the minds of many Americans with the massive influx of southern and eastern Europeans at the turn of the century. Since the late 1960s, America has again become a country of large-scale immigration, this time attracting newcomers from developing societies of the world. The number of foreign-born is at an all-time high: nearly 20 million foreign-born persons were counted in the 1990 census. Although immigrants are a smaller share of the nation's population than they were earlier in the century—8 percent in 1990 compared to about 15 percent in 1910—recent immigrants are having an especially dramatic impact because their geographic concentration is greater today. About half of all immigrants entering the United States during the 1980s moved to eight urban areas: Los Angeles, New York, Miami, Anaheim, Chicago, Washington, D.C., Houston, and San Francisco. America's major urban centers are, increasingly, immigrant cities with new ethnic mixes.

Who are the new immigrants? What are their lives like here? How are they redefining themselves and their cultures? And how are they contributing to a new and changing America? The *New Immigrants Series* provides a set of case studies that explores these themes among a variety of groups. Each book in the series is written by a recognized expert who has done extensive in-depth ethnographic research on one of the immigrant groups. The groups represent a broad range of today's arrivals, coming from a variety of countries and cultures. The studies cover a wide geographical range as well, based on research done in different parts of the country, from New York to California.

Most of the books in the series are written by anthropologists. All draw on qualitative research that shows what it means to be an immigrant in America today. As part of each study, individual immigrants tell their stories, which will help give a sense of the experiences and problems of the newcomers. Through the case studies, a dynamic picture emerges of the way immigrants are carving out new lives for themselves at the same time as they are creating a new and more diverse America.

The ethnographic case study, long the anthropologist's trademark, provides a depth often lacking in research on immigrants in the United States. Many anthropologists, moreover, like a number of authors in the *New Immigrants Series*, have done research in the sending society as well as in the United States. Having field experience at both ends of the migration chain makes anthropologists particularly sensitive to the role of transnational ties that link immigrants to their home societies. With first-hand experience of immigrants in their home culture, anthropologists are also well positioned to appreciate continuities as well as changes in the immigrant setting.

As the United States faces a growing backlash against immigration, and many Americans express ambivalence and sometimes hostility toward the latest arrivals, it becomes more important than ever to learn about the new immigrants and to hear their voices. The case studies in the *New Immigrants Series* will help readers understand the cultures and lives of the newest Americans and bring out the complex ways the newcomers are coming to terms with and creatively adapting to life in a new land.

NANCY FONER
Series Editor

Acknowledgments

I am deeply grateful to the following persons for assisting me or commenting on this book: Professor Pham Cao Duong; Ann Freeman; Patricia Freeman; Julie Hoang, Research Analyst, Department of Finance, Demographic Research Unit, State of California; Co T. Nguyen, Vice President, *Nguoi Viet*; Huu Dinh Nguyen, M.S.W., Executive Director, Aid to Children without Parents; Minh-Hoang N. Nguyen, M.S.W., Psychiatric Social Worker, Santa Clara County, California Mental Health; Nguyen Huynh Mai; Rosy N.Tran, M.S.-MFCC, Santa Clara County, California Mental Health; Tran Van Tai; Usha Welaratna; and finally the many persons who kindly agreed to be interviewed for this book.

I thank Stanford University Press for letting me quote from my book, *Hearts of Sorrow: Vietnamese-American Lives* (1989), and I am grateful to Minh Huynh and *Suvannabhumi*, Newsletter of the Program for the Southeast Asian Studies at Arizona State University, for permission to quote from Huynh's article, "Plant Care and Americanization: A Personal View," Volume 6, Number 2, May 1995.

Introducing Vietnamese Americans

In the early morning hours of April 30, 1975, a sea of fleeing refugees surged around the walls of the U.S.Embassy in
Saigon. The South had lost the war in Vietnam. North Vietnamese troops were nearing Saigon, and the terrified inhab-
itants were desperately seeking to escape, hoping that the
Americans would help them.

One man who was there, Colonel Nguyen Dinh Khanh of
the South Vietnamese army, recalls those final hours. As he
pushed his way towards the fence of the U.S. embassy, Colonel Khanh clutched an old letter written by an American lieu-
tenant general commending the colonel for his work with the
Americans. The colonel showed it to the Marine guard on
duty and asked to be let in, along with his family. The guard
told him to try to get in by the rear gate. For several hours
they went around the Embassy in vain attempts to push
through the densely packed crowd. Finally they gave up and
went home. The colonel's friend, Dr. Ho Van Cham, the Min-
ister of Information, tried to climb the Embassy fence. A Marine guard smashed him in the head with the butt end of his
gun, and he fell back bleeding. Neither Colonel Khanh nor
Dr. Cham escaped; several weeks later the North Vietnamese
sent them off to harsh jungle prisons called reeducation
camps, where for years they endured starvation, hard labor,

abuse, and humiliating treatment (Aurora Foundation 1989; Freeman 1989: 201-270).

Colonel Khanh and Dr. Cham were among the thousands of Vietnamese promised safe haven but abandoned by the Americans on that fateful April morning. As dawn broke, the last American helicopters lifted off from the top roof of the U.S. Embassy; they took with them the last American and a handful of the thousands of panicked Vietnamese people clamoring to escape (Butler 1985: 443-452, photos between 178-179; Isaacs 1983: 447-487; Karnow: 668-669).

In the chaotic final days of the war, an estimated 135,000 Vietnamese people fled their homeland. Nearly 5,600 were airlifted out by U.S. military aircraft to offshore U.S. naval vessels; the others fled to these ships in small boats. In the days that followed, thousands more made their way by small boat to nearby countries. Most of these people were military personnel and government officials of the Republic of Vietnam and their families, or others who had been associated with the American involvement in Vietnam. Those fortunate enough to escape were processed in transit camps and then dispersed throughout the United States. But large numbers of high risk potential victims of Communist persecution were left behind. These included 1.5 million soldiers, police, and civil service of the defeated South Vietnamese government, two thirds of the 90,000 Vietnamese and their families who had been employees of the American embassy, countless others who had worked for the CIA, and an estimated 30,000 counterterrorist agents. These people were made especially vulnerable because the United States, "committed that unpardonable mistake of failing to ensure the destruction of the personnel files and intelligence dossiers...which identified so many of those left on the tarmac or outside the gates of the embassy" (Snepp 1978: 565-567). Most were put in reeducation camps, where they remained for three to fifteen years. After their release or escape, thousands, like Colonel Khanh, fled Vietnam and came to America as refugees.

Although a few thousand people from Vietnam, Laos, and Cambodia had come to the United States before 1975, the end of the war and the Communist takeover of their countries marks the beginning of the massive migration of these peoples to America. This book focuses on the Vietnamese, the largest of these three groups to arrive on American shores. According to the U.S. Department of State, from April 1975 through September 1994, about 1.32 million people from Laos, Cambodia, and Vietnam have come to live in the United States. Of these, more than 900,000 are Vietnamese. With their children born in the United States, the total number of Vietnamese in America is now over one million.

Most of the Vietnamese, about 700,000, have come to the United States as refugees, that is, as persons who were forced to flee their homelands, often for their lives. They were persecuted or feared being persecuted on account of their ethnic, religious, or political affiliations. They included dissenters persecuted for their expressed beliefs or actions, members of specific groups singled out for persecution, and people who fled because they became inadvertent or random victims of violence or persecution. Many made no real preparations for migrating and had no idea where they would go; their only thought was to escape, often at great risk to their lives. They left everything behind: home, country, family, friends, work, material possessions, social status, and meaningful sources of identity. Most of them believed that they would never be able to return to Vietnam without risking imprisonment or death. Although the Socialist Republic of Vietnam now encourages Vietnamese to visit their native land, some former refugees, fearing persecution, still refuse to do so. Before 1980, Vietnamese refugees were admitted into the United States under special parole (refugee granting) powers of the U.S. President and through special short-term legislation. Since 1980, many Vietnamese refugees have been admitted under the Refugee Act of 1980.

The United States government gives refugees various kinds of temporary public assistance. The funds to help refugees have been made available through laws voted on by the U.S. Congress. The aim is to enable refugees to become economically self-sufficient as quickly as possible. Many Vietnamese refugees have used this assistance, which has included English instruction, job training, health coverage, and living expenses. Although programs to assist refugees have been sharply reduced over the years from thirty-six months of support to eight months, they have played an important role in helping refugees adjust to life in America.

Since 1980, more than 200,000 Vietnamese have come to America, not as refugees, but as legal immigrants. Unlike refugees, they have deliberately chosen to come to a new life and have prepared for living in America. In most cases, they have been sponsored by relatives already residing in the United States. Most of these people have been admitted to the United States under a special program called the Orderly Departure Program (ODP). This was established by the United Nations High Commission for Refugees to provide a means for Vietnamese to leave their country and resettle without having to attempt dangerous escapes. As a rule, unlike refugees these immigrants are not entitled to the same forms of public assistance; their sponsors are responsible for taking care of them. But there are some exceptions: some people have refused to assist their newly arrived relatives, who then turn to public assistance. Some former political and reeducation camp prisoners also receive public assistance. They and their families emigrate to the United States on another special program called the Humanitarian Operation (HO), or Special Released Reeducation Center Detainee Resettlement Program. This program was established in 1987 by an agreement signed by the U.S. and Vietnam. To qualify, former prisoners must prove that they had been in reeducation camps for three years or longer. A third special program, begun in 1988, is the Amerasian Homecoming Program. This allows for admission of Amerasians and their families. Amerasians are the children of Vietnamese mothers and U.S. citizens (Le Ngoan 1994: 2).

VIETNAMESE AMERICANS, ASIAN AMERICANS, AND OTHER REFUGEES AND IMMIGRANTS

The people of Vietnam are diverse, consisting of 54 distinct ethnic groups. By far the largest of these groups, both in Vietnam and in America, is the Viet or Kinh. In this book, I use the term Vietnamese American to refer to any of the people from Vietnam who live in America, as well as their children born in the United States. Although the term Vietnamese American is in wide use, there is no consensus on how the Vietnamese in America refer to themselves. They call themselves Vietnamese, Vietnamese American, and American. In different situations, they may refer to themselves by the smaller ethnic categories by which they are known in Vietnam.

The Vietnamese typically use a different word order for their names than do Americans. Colonel Nguyen Dinh Khanh's surname is Nguyen; his personal name is Khanh. The custom is to refer to him by his title and his first name, Colonel Khanh. In the United States, a number of Vietnamese have reversed this order to conform with American usage, thus Colonel Khanh Dinh Nguyen. I use the word order that people themselves have requested. To protect their privacy, I have used pseudonyms except for public figures and those who specifically requested that their names be used.

Sociologist Ruben Rumbaut notes that Vietnamese, Laotian, and Cambodian Americans, despite some differences, share several distinctive characteristics. First, unlike other Asians in America, most came to the United States as refugees rather than immigrants. Second, as refugees, and unlike immigrants, many received the special public assistance mentioned previously. Third, unlike other Asian Americans, they are all new arrivals, with no settled communities of previous migrants from their countries to welcome them. Fourth, except for the Vietnamese refugees of 1975, they tend to be less well educated and more rural than other Asian immigrant groups over the past several decades. Finally, they are a relatively young population. These characteristics affect their adjustments in America (Rumbaut 1995: 232-233; Hein 1993 and Le Ngoan 1994: 7).

All three groups were traumatized by their war and refugee experiences but in different ways. For the Vietnamese, the defining experience is often said to be their escape by boat. In the years following the Communist takeover of their country, well over one million Vietnamese attempted perilous escapes by boat; the majority fled between 1978 and 1982. Their journeys, often in small, unseaworthy vessels, lasted from a couple of days to weeks, and the distances they traveled ranged from a few hundred miles to five thousand miles. Tens of thousands died; the estimates range from ten to fifty percent. The survivors weathered fierce storms, attacks by Vietnamese patrols near Vietnam and by pirates out at sea; they suffered from hunger, thirst, and dehydration. Still others fled overland from Vietnam through Cambodia, hoping to reach Thailand. They were hunted by bandits, Khmer Rouge soldiers, and Vietnamese troops. Thousands died in transit.

The survivors, both of overland and boat escapes, were placed in harsh, brutal refugee camps in countries of first asylum for periods ranging from one to several years. There is hardly a Vietnamese family in the United States today that does not have at least one member who arrived as a boat person or overland escapee, or who died or disappeared en route. These collective experiences, and the stories that surround them, make up an important part of Vietnamese-American identity.

Upon arrival in the United States, the Vietnamese received a mixed reception. Because of the Vietnam War, many people opened their arms to provide assistance and to help the newly arrived Vietnamese adjust to the United States. But the war also prompted the opposite response; some people resented the presence of the Vietnamese, associating them with a failed and unpopular war that had cost American lives and had deeply divided the nation. They also faced confrontations based on anti-immigrant sentiments, which have grown over the years as Vietnamese refugees and immigrants have continued to arrive in the United States.

Vietnamese Americans share with many other refugee groups certain characteristics that affect how they cope with life in the United States. Because of war, many groups, including the Vietnamese, have ambivalent attitudes towards their homeland. The Vietnam war was a shattering experience that disrupted families and traditions. For those who remained for a while under Communist rule, the reforms of the new regime were equally if not more disruptive. Understandably, Vietnamese refugees often express strong anti-Communist sentiments, and many vigorously opposed the resumption of diplomatic relations with the Socialist Republic of Vietnam. At the same time, these new refugees retain a strong sentimental attachment to their homeland, customs, and traditions, and to the many relatives they left behind in Vietnam, including those who fought on the other side of the war. Over the years, Vietnamese Americans have sent money and medicines, now estimated at 700 million to one billion dollars a year, to help support their impoverished relatives in Vietnam.

Some Vietnamese also have mixed reactions about living in the United States, a country which abandoned them at war's end, but then took them in as refugees, giving them political freedom and new educational and economic opportunities. A former South Vietnamese captain and reeducation camp prisoner, now in America, says, "A lot of Vietnamese believed that we lost because the Americans withdrew their military aid in 1973...I figured that we had been betrayed and abandoned" (Freeman 1989: 266-267). A middle-aged woman says, "The United States caused us to lose the war. Then they turned their backs on us. Even though I worked for them, they left me behind. I went through nine years of hell under the Communists before I was able to get out."

While grateful to America, older Vietnamese fear that living in America leads to the loss and abandonment of their traditions. An elderly Vietnamese refugee told me, "We are reluctant to express these views. But poetry reflects our true feelings. Ha Huyen Chi writes, 'Your father has two enemies, Communists and Americans.'" ["Father" refers to Vietnamese culture.] "Why, then, do you stay here?" I asked the professor. He replied, "We have no choice. The Vietnamese have learned endurance. We are like the Vietnamese rickshaw man who pulls for twelve kilometers without stop, even though the end is terrible; like him, we have no choice."

Like other refugee and immigrant groups, the Vietnamese are attached to traditions and their remembered life in their ancestral land. This book will examine some of these traditions to see how they affect Vietnamese adjustments in the United States. For example, the Vietnamese place a high value on nurturing and supportive families, in which the parents' sacrifices for their children are reciprocated by obligations children fulfill for their parents. The Vietnamese also value education. Their heroes are scholars as well as warriors.

The Vietnamese take great pride in their ancient history. Each
year, in Vietnamese communities throughout America, celebrations are held in honor of Hung Vuong, the mythical first
ruler of Vietnam who is said to have lived 4,000 years ago,
and the Trung sisters, who led a revolt against the Chinese
nearly 2,000 years ago. Many Vietnamese Americans, even
though they lived in cities in Vietnam, trace their roots back
to villages. Now, living in the United States, they romanticize
village life as idyllic. They return to Vietnam to visit family
tombs and pay respects to their ancestors.

Americans tend to view the Vietnamese as homogeneous
and overlook important differences among them. In addition
to age, gender, and family background, other sources of vari-
ation include urban or rural background, ethnicity (Viet or
Kinh, Chinese, Cambodian, Tribal, or Cham—the descendants of an Indianized kingdom of central and south Vietnam), social class, region of the country, religion (Buddhist,
Catholic, and indigenous developments such as Hoa Hao
Buddhist and Cao Dai), and the year and type of their refugee
flight or immigration to the United States.

Like many immigrant and refugee groups, Vietnamese
ethnic groups find that other Americans do not know much
about them; the Viet or Kinh are frequently confused with the
Chinese. The Viet see themselves as a unique people with a
common language and shared values. They are proud of their
historical roots, significant achievements, and successful resistance to Chinese and other invaders. Other ethnic groups
from Vietnam do not necessarily share the values of the Viet
(Hickey 1982a: 385-437; 1982b: entire). They are typically confused with the Viet and their identity as ethnic minorities is
frequently unknown to Americans (Antypa 1994).

During times of economic downturn in American communities, Vietnamese Americans, along with other refugees
and immigrants, typically find themselves blamed for crises
they do not cause. Often they are accused of being welfare
sponges and members of gangs, or of taking away jobs from
others. Vietnamese Americans have been accused of getting
special favors and privileges denied other groups, such as interest-free loans for houses and cars. As anti-immigrant sentiment grows and ethnic hostilities escalate, people question

the right of the Vietnamese to be in the United States. They are accused of being "economic migrants" who simply came to America seeking jobs rather than as refugees fleeing for their lives. When they succeed in school or work, they hear accusations that they used unfair means to get ahead. And because many have been successful, the misconception has arisen that Vietnamese Americans, along with some other Asian groups, have no need of special services.

This book will show why these statements are misleading. Vietnamese Americans have been legally admitted to the United States as refugees or immigrants. Families buy houses and cars by saving their money and pooling resources, not by receiving interest-free loans. Their successes have come through initiative, a work ethic, respect for education and skills, and an innovativeness that fit right in with American ideals.

Although not representative of the community as a whole, gangs are a problem for the Vietnamese, as is the continuing poverty of some families. Newly arrived refugees and immigrants often live in disintegrating neighborhoods, with poor schools and widespread unemployment. Previously their lives had been violated in their homelands; their lives, and their right to live without fear, continue to be violated in the United States. In this the Vietnamese are not unique. The problems they face are the result of poverty-stricken environments that plague all groups who live in these circumstances.

Many Vietnamese are struggling to make ends meet. Some of these people receive public assistance or welfare. Most eventually find jobs and become economically self-sufficient. Far from competing for scarce jobs, many Vietnamese, including those who were highly educated and well-off in their homeland, have taken demeaning jobs that many Americans reject. Those who succeed do so through hard work and the support of their families. As Vietnamese businesses expand, they are hiring people of many different ethnic backgrounds, providing new job opportunities for others, not taking them away. As their length of residence in the U.S. increases, the incomes earned by the Vietnamese increase and their use of public assistance declines (Hein 1993: 56-58; Le Ngoan 1994: 13).

VIETNAMESE COMMUNITIES IN AMERICA

When the Vietnamese first arrived in the United States, the government dispersed them throughout the country so that they would not be concentrated in one or two places and so that the financial burdens of resettlement and the demands on state and county would be distributed evenly. The new refugees were sponsored by individuals, churches, and voluntary organizations, many of them in small towns. More than two-thirds of the Vietnamese began their life in America in communities in which there were under 500 refugees. By 1990, many had moved to states where the climate was warmer, jobs were more plentiful, and larger Vietnamese communities were forming. Those who have moved from their original place of resettlement are called secondary migrants.

Most of the early boat people were ethnic Chinese; as soon as they could, they went to live in urban Chinatowns throughout the United States. Other early refugees included fishermen who had ready access to boats along the Vietnamese coast. In America, they relocated to Gulf Coast cities as well as to towns in California where they could pursue economic opportunities related to fishing. Other refugees moved near Washington D.C., as well as to cities such as Chicago, Seattle, Houston, and New Orleans. But the largest number of secondary migrants headed for California, which now is home to over half of all Southeast Asian refugees in America (California Department of Finance 1994: 1; see also U.S. Department of Commerce, Bureau of the Census 1990d and 1990e for additional statistical information on California).

According to the 1990 census, 614,547 persons in America are of Vietnamese descent, of whom about 110,000 individuals or 18 percent were born in the United States. These figures are well below the number of actual arrivals from Vietnam recorded by the U.S. State Department and the Office of Refugee Resettlement. The figures appear to exclude up to 200,000 persons from Vietnam who identified themselves as Chinese for the census. Furthermore, leaders in several communities contend that other Vietnamese also were not counted. Although the Bureau of the Census initially rejected such claims, it now estimates that it undercounted Asians by 3 percent (Epstein 1995: 6A). Other studies point to undercounting. In 1994, the National Congress of Vietnamese in America estimated the number of Vietnamese in America to be 900,000.

Of the total population of Vietnamese Americans listed by the 1990 census, 280,223 persons, or 45.6 percent live in California. Texas, with 69,636 (11.3 percent) and Virginia, with 20,693 (3.4 percent) follow. Other states in excess of 10,000 Vietnamese Americans include Washington (18,696), Florida (16,646), Pennsylvania (15,887), New York (15,555), Massachusetts (15,449), and Illinois (10,309). In Orange County, California, a Los Angeles Times poll of 1989 estimated that over 100,000 Vietnamese lived in that county; the 1990 Census counted only 71,822 (Cluck 1994: 19; Le Ngoan 1994: 2-6; see also U.S. Department of Commerce, Bureau of the Census 1990a, 1990b, 1990c for additional statistical information).

Whatever the correct figures, there is no doubt that the highest concentration of Vietnamese is in Southern California's Orange and Los Angeles Counties, followed by the Northern California County of Santa Clara, centered around the city of San Jose, in the heart of "Silicon Valley." In Orange County, the Vietnamese cluster especially in the towns of Garden Grove, Santa Ana, Anaheim, and Westminster, a small community which contains a shopping area officially called Little Saigon. Vietnamese from towns all over Southern California come to Little Saigon to shop or simply to stroll through ornate shopping malls and centers, where they find Vietnamese book and video stores, travel agencies that book flights to Vietnam, pharmacies that sell Chinese herbs and medicines, noodle shops and restaurants which specialize in Vietnamese regional dishes, night clubs and karaoke spots, grocery stores offering an array of Asian foods, and the offices of physicians, dentists, tax accountants, and lawyers, as well as those of community service agencies and refugee rights advocacy groups (Karnow 1993: 31-32). During celebrations such as the Vietnamese New Year, Little Saigon stores carry special cakes of rice and pork wrapped and steamed in banana leaves, and a wide variety of sweets.

Little Saigon is home to eight Vietnamese newspapers, including *Nguoi Viet* (Vietnamese People), founded in 1978, the largest Vietnamese newspaper in America. Some newspapers are distributed free; their earnings come from advertising. Numerous magazines and literary journals, such as The *Ky 21* (The 21st Century), also come from Little Saigon. Santa Ana, in Orange County, houses Little Saigon T.V. and Little Saigon Radio, which reaches over 200,000 listeners. And Orange County is the center of Vietnamese-American music, video, and literary productions.

Sociologist Steven Gold suggests that the development of an enclave such as Little Saigon fulfills important needs for some Vietnamese people. Businesses in areas like Little Saigon were often started by people "who spoke little English and maintained minimum contact with American society," and in some cases wanted to keep it that way. Gold talked with Vietnamese people who told him that they preferred to limit their contacts with an unfamiliar culture, to provide employment for relatives and provide a positive setting for their families to develop in the United States, and finally, to enjoy the relationships that come from living and working within the refugee community and immersing themselves in Vietnamese culture (Gold 1992: 175-176). In Little Saigon, they can speak the Vietnamese language, retain old customs, and interact with people with whom they share common values and feel at ease. However, those who spend all their time in Little Saigon are mostly the elderly as well as some new arrivals.

Even those who do not live in the area return to Little Saigon to be reinvigorated. One refugee said, "I have a successful business, and I hire mostly non-Vietnamese employees. I work hard all week. Neither my business nor my home are near Little Saigon. But when the weekend comes, I want to go to Little Saigon, see a little bit of Vietnamese culture, drink some coffee, eat some noodle soup, meet old friends, and listen to them 'yak yak yak.' Then I feel good and at ease again."

There is no single typical Vietnamese community in America. Communities vary in size and the quality of life they offer. Little Saigon, notes journalist Lowell Weiss, is a place where shopkeepers and professionals reinvest much of their profits; they have a huge stake in keeping it safe and clean. It is an area that has provided excellent employment, as well as a warm reception by conservative Americans, for refugees fleeing Communism. Weiss contrasts this with Dorchester, in metropolitan Boston, which contains a Vietnamese community of around five thousand people. "As soon as refugees begin to earn a decent living, they flee the low-rent Vietnamese hub in the Dorchester section of the city...Unlike Little Saigon, the Dorchester enclave feels at once depressed and tense. Not only has it been left to the most vulnerable refugees; it is also an inner city melting pot of blacks, Latinos, and Irish-Americans which is often on the verge of boiling over. Unemployment among the Dorchester Vietnamese is high, approximately 20 percent—50 percent if one includes all those who are still receiving federal refugee assistance checks. There are few Vietnamese-owned businesses, and those that exist almost never hire people outside the proprietor's family" (Weiss 1994: 36).

The Vietnamese of inner-city Philadelphia, 6,000-10,000 in number, face similar problems: in the mid-1980s, when sociologist Nazli Kibria conducted her study, they were newly arrived refugees, resettled in an inexpensive urban area in which poverty and unemployment far exceeded national rates. "Unlike the large Vietnamese immigrant settlements in Southern California or Virginia, the one in Philadelphia was neither highly visible nor clearly bounded, and it did not have a core geographical center....the prevalent pattern was of small clusters of Vietnamese American settlement rather than dominance over a large area." The Vietnamese lived next to other racial/ethnic groups, "including blacks, Koreans, Indians, Chinese, and Ethiopians, as well as the various Southeast Asian refugee groups" (Kibria 1993: 25). Because of intergroup hostilities, a high crime rate, and poor schools in the area, the families whom Kibria studied did not consider this low-rent area a desirable place to live, and they moved out when they had the means to do so. While they had informal social networks based on kin and friends in different neighborhoods, they lacked the cohesiveness of Little Saigon. Philadelphia Vietnamese were distrustful of Vietnamese ethnic organizations which competed with one another, and their involvement with religious organizations was limited (Kibria 1993: 26-27).

HOW THIS BOOK CAME TO BE WRITTEN

In 1980, I became aware that San Jose, California, where I live, was undergoing dramatic transformation with the influx of thousands of Vietnamese refugees, about whom little was known. The story of the Vietnamese is particularly compelling because of the U.S. involvement in the Vietnam war. This story touches deeply the lives of Americans as well as those of the refugees themselves. Since 1980, I have done research and community service and advocacy involving Indochinese refugees. I have used participant observation and interviewed Vietnamese people in several sites in the United States, though mainly in California. Between 1991 and 1994, as officer of Aid to Children Without Parents, Inc. (ACWP), a nonprofit organization that assists refugee children, I visited thirteen refugee camps in Hong Kong, Thailand, Malaysia, the Philippines, Singapore, and Indonesia, where I observed and interviewed children and their guardians as well as government and United Nations officials. In 1993 and 1994, at the invitation of the Vietnamese government, I went to Vietnam with ACWP to set up a project, now in operation, to assist orphans and repatriated unaccompanied minors. I observed and interviewed children throughout Vietnam. I also traveled with several Vietnamese Americans who were visiting Vietnam for the first time since they had fled as refugees. When not traveling, I stayed with a poor family in Saigon. I have drawn on these experiences in the writing of this book. I have also drawn on my personal experiences. I come from a European immigrant extended family that was disrupted by war. My maternal grandfather, as a prisoner of war, was incarcerated for seven years in a Siberian mining labor camp; my mother and her elder brother spent the formative years of their childhood without a father, traumatized in a house occupied by foreign troops. My grandfather escaped from Siberia and brought his family to America. Of our seventy-eight relatives who remained in Europe, only three survived. These family memories have helped me to understand Vietnamese accounts of family disruption, political reeducation camps, migration to a new land, and also the difficulties of striving to survive in a new land.

As you read about the people in this book, a good question to ask yourself is how your own experiences compare or differ with theirs. You might try to understand what the world, and the United States, looks like to these people. In what ways are their views similar or different from those of other groups in the United States, and why? As the author introducing these people and their culture to you, my aim is to give you some details about them, but equally important to convey the spirit of these people, the distinctive elements and patterns of their lives that make them Vietnamese Americans.

2

Historical Roots of the Vietnamese Refugee Exodus

Vietnamese culture began over four thousand years ago near the Red River in north Vietnam. In 111 B.C., the Vietnamese came under the control of the Chinese, who ruled them for over one thousand years until they were forced out in 939 A.D. Vietnamese civilization blends both Chinese and indigenous Vietnamese features. From China came Confucianism, Buddhism, and Taoism. From Vietnam came folk beliefs and practices, egalitarian village ways, and greater independence of women than is found in Chinese ideology (Jamieson 1993; Taylor 1993).

Vietnamese history is marked by turbulent revolts and wars against China, and wars against Champa, an Indianized empire which for 1500 years ruled central and south Vietnam. Despite the devastation caused by these conflicts, the Vietnamese remained in their homeland. In 1975, the Communists took control of south Vietnam, and for the first time in Vietnamese history, large numbers of people fled beyond the Indochinese peninsula. This unprecedented event was the end result of nearly a century of drastic changes in Vietnamese society starting with the French occupation of the country.

When the French gained control of Vietnam in the second half of the 19th century, they encountered a Confucian court which discouraged commerce, new ideas, and diversity and underestimated the wealth, power, and determination of the foreigners. Traditionalists who resisted the French were overwhelmed by the changes that were introduced: opening up Vietnam to Catholic missionaries; instituting excessive taxes; establishing monopolies for the sale, at exorbitant prices, of salt, opium (previously prohibited by Vietnamese rulers), and alcohol (which people were forced to buy); collecting land and individual or body taxes; and using forced labor to mine coal, tin, and zinc and develop commercial agriculture.

Historian Joseph Buttinger concludes, "The Vietnamese people, direct objects of exploitation, gained nothing at all under the colonial regime. On the contrary, there is much evidence that for the majority life was harder in 1930 than it had been a hundred years earlier" (Buttinger 1972: 65-69; see also Ngo Vinh Long 1991; Duiker 1995a: 26-36; Duiker 1995b: 11-15). Duiker observes that French ways conflicted with Confucian institutions and values. Confucian values emphasized the subordination of the individual to the family and community; the French emphasized individual freedom. The Vietnamese world view, like the Chinese, stressed harmony with nature; the French "glorified the conquest of nature," change and progress. French education especially exerted a "corrosive impact on Vietnamese institutions, values, and culture." A newly emergent urban middle class imitated French customs, habits, and dress, entered Western professions such as engineering, medicine, and law, and imitated Western trends in art, music, literature (Duiker 1995a: 175-179).

RESISTANCE AND WAR

Vietnamese resistance to the French began in the early days of colonial rule, first from traditionalists who wished to restore the traditional Confucian Vietnamese state, later from those who used Western practices against the French. This resistance coalesced in the 1920s with the rise of the Indochinese Communist party, led by Ho Chi Minh (Marr 1971; 1981).

In 1941, the Indochinese Communist Party formed the Viet Minh as an organization to bring about national liberation. To draw support from a wide spectrum of Vietnamese and to consolidate many groups, the Viet Minh leaders spoke of patriotic national resistance to the French rather than Communist social and economic reforms (Duiker 1995: 22-24; Pike 1966: 3-24). Many young people were drawn to the movement without realizing its ultimate aims; some later became disillusioned, withdrew, and opposed the Communists. At the end of the Vietnam war, some of these people fearing persecution from the Communists, fled as refugees and now reside in the United States (Freeman 1989: 124-135).

Between 1940 and 1945, the Japanese seized control of Indochina by force as part of their expansion during World War II. throughout Asia and the Pacific. At first, the Japanese left the French colonial administration in place, but in 1945, the Japanese deposed the French and replaced them with a pro-Japanese puppet government under the Vietnamese emperor Bao Dai. This destroyed French control in the countryside, and the Viet Minh, along with other anticolonial nationalist organizations, moved in to seize the rural areas (Duiker 1995a: 43-45). Peasants were receptive to the Viet Minh, especially in north Vietnam, where the Japanese caused a terrible famine by forcing peasants to grow cash crops and keeping rice for their own troops, refusing to release food stores, and destroying much of this food when they were defeated. The French also contributed to this famine by confiscating rice. A Catholic priest recalls that he and his family survived by concealing rice in covered jars, buried in the ground and covered with grass. Ravenous peasants streamed into towns seeking food; thousands died on the streets. Two million people died of starvation (Freeman 1989: 118-120).

After the defeat of the Japanese, the Viet Minh declared Vietnam's independence from the French in the August Revolution of 1945, and within two weeks controlled most of north and central Vietnam, especially the rural areas. The French, aided by the British and the Americans, refused to relinquish their colonial empire. Thus began the 30-year conflict for the control of Vietnam, first between the Vietnamese Communists and other groups against the French, later between the Vietnamese Communists of north and south Vietnam against the Vietnamese Nationalists of the South, aided mainly by the Americans. By 1946, many of the non-Communist Vietnamese leaders and organizations had been eliminated either by the Viet Minh or by the French, and in December 1946, the Viet Minh launched attacks against the French.

By 1953, as the fighting continued without resolution, antiwar public opinion increased in France. Meanwhile, the United States stepped up its involvement; it was concerned that the Chinese Communists were helping the Viet Minh and feared that a Viet Minh victory would lead to a Communist takeover of neighboring countries. By the end of 1953, the United States was paying two thirds of the cost of the war.

In May 1954, the Viet Minh won a major victory at Dien Bien Phu, near the Laotian border, just as international peace talks on Vietnam were about to begin in Geneva. These talks led to an agreement to establish a temporary division of Vietnam into two zones, divided at the 17th Parallel, with general elections to be held in both zones in July 1956. The two zones became the Democratic Republic of Vietnam in the North and the Republic of Vietnam (or Government of Vietnam) in the South. France withdrew from Indochina, but the United States, which would not accept the possibility of a Communist election, refused to sign the Geneva accords, and the elections were never held. For about a year after the Geneva accords, people who wished to relocate from one zone to another were allowed to do so. Many Communists moved to the North. A larger number of north Vietnamese, nearly one million and some say two million, moved to the South. Many were helped by the U.S. Navy in their evacuation.

In the South a new government was formed with Ngo Dinh Diem as president. A Catholic from a traditional elite family, Ngo Dinh Diem was ardently anti-French and anti-Communist. While initially supported by the United States, Ngo Dinh Diem's government gradually deteriorated. Opposition centered around the alienation of rural peoples, the suppression of dissent, especially Buddhist protests, and alleged government favoritism of Catholics. In 1963, with the assent of the United States, he was overthrown and assassinated in a military coup. Under American support, a succession of military leaders assumed the presidency until the fall of South Vietnam in 1975.

Meanwhile, starting in 1959, the North Vietnamese sent southerners to infiltrate the Government of Vietnam in the South. They had been trained in the North. In 1960, they founded the National Front for the Liberation of Vietnam (NLF), directed by the North, but appearing to be a spontaneous movement of a wide spectrum of South Vietnamese Buddhists, peasants, intellectuals, minority peoples, and others (Pike 1966: 37-44). The NLF was the public political facade of the Viet Cong, comprised of many Southern Communists, but with Northern Communist cadres in key leadership positions. (Swearington and Rolf 1967: 82-83). South Vietnamese typically used the term Viet Cong to refer to all Communists, those from the North as well as the South.

In 1964, the North sent their troops into the South. By that time, many of the rural areas were under the control of the Communists. President Lyndon Johnson responded by requesting Congress to pass the Gulf of Tonkin Resolution, which gave the President broad powers to expand the U.S. military role in Vietnam. The United States hoped to strengthen the Government of Vietnam and prevent Communist victory. Over the next three years, as the war escalated, opposition to it mounted in the United States, especially on university campuses.

In January 1968, during the Tet or New Year's holidays, the Communists launched an offensive in the countryside and in many cities, including Saigon and Hue, where some 10,000 persons, nearly half of them civilians, lost their lives. Two thirds of Hue was totally destroyed, and 90,000 people out of the population of 130,000 were made refugees (Jamieson 1991: 321; Pham Van Son 1968: 56). Although the Communists were beaten back in all areas and lost 60,000 men, perhaps half of their assault force, the Tet Offensive is considered by many to be a watershed event and a psychological victory for the Communists, since it turned American public opinion more solidly against continuation of the war (Pham Van Son 1968: 55-57). American forces were gradually withdrawn, and in January 1973, after prolonged negotiations with North Vietnam, the United States agreed to a cease fire and the removal of remaining U.S. troops. Still, the North attacked and the South fought back. In the Spring of 1975, the Communists launched their final offensive. By that time, the United States not only had removed their fighting forces and cut their military aid to South Vietnam but also refused to honor President Nixon's promise to respond militarily if the Communists attacked. South Vietnam's resistance collapsed, and Saigon fell on April 30.

The war's toll was enormous. Between 1945 and 1975, over three million Vietnamese soldiers and civilians on both sides were killed. Between 1961 and 1973, the period of active military involvement of the United States, the number of military dead included nearly 58,000 American soldiers and more than 200,000 South Vietnamese soldiers. Between 1954 and 1975, an estimated 1.1 million soldiers from North Vietnam and the National Liberation Front (South Vietnamese Communists) were killed, including 300,000 missing in action. Another 600,000 were wounded. Nearly two million civilians were killed in the North and South, and about the same number were injured (Indochina Interchange 1995: 29; Ministry of Labor, War Invalids, and Social Affairs 1995).

For the United States, the military cost of the war was 165 billion dollars. Between 1955 and 1975, an additional 24 billion dollars in aid was given to South Vietnam. With their victory in 1975, the Communists seized U.S.military equipment worth one billion dollars. More than 5 billion dollars in military hardware supplied to the South Vietnamese government was lost, enough "to field an entire army, air force or navy" (Snepp 1978: 567-568).

As a consequence of the war, the United States suffered inflation and economic dislocations, we well as disillusion with a failed foreign policy and leaders who had drawn the nation into an unpopular war. But for Vietnam, North as well as South, the social, economic, and ecological effects were far more devastating: 8.5 million people were relocated from South Vietnam alone, families were separated, 800,000 children were orphaned, forests were incinerated, 5.2 million acres were defoliated, agricultural lands were contaminated, whole villages disappeared.

SORROWS OF LIBERATION

The destruction continued long after the Vietnam war ended. America's post-war trade embargo of Vietnam, and Vietnam's own repressive post-war economic and social policies, including the persecution of hundreds of thousands of individuals, continued to disrupt the fabric of Vietnamese society. A few weeks after the Communist victory in South Vietnam, the new government ordered several hundred thousand former South Vietnamese soldiers and government officials to report for ten days to two weeks of political instruction. When they arrived, they were hustled off to reeducation camps, where they were starved, demeaned, forced to do heavy physical labor, and were subjected to political indoctrination, including forced confessions of real and imaginary crimes against the Communists. Incarceration lasted anywhere from a few months to fifteen years or more. Thousands died of starvation, disease, and abuse, and some were executed for breaking rules or trying to escape. The families of these prisoners were torn apart, and some wives abandoned their husbands.

One former prisoner described to me how some men coped with gnawing hunger. When one of his friends found a mouse nest with four or five newly born still-red mice, "he picked them up, stuck them on an improvised stick of bamboo, and ate them raw right there....Most of the men ate what they could find, such as small frogs the size of your thumb...pulling out their entrails, tearing off their skin, and eating them raw. They also ate live crickets, first pulling off their spiny legs, then popping the crickets in their mouths" (Freeman 1989: 232).

Another prisoner described what happened to the men when they suffered work injuries which became infected. "The amputation of limbs was done with a handsaw, without anesthesia....Everyone in the camp heard their terrible screams. Then their stumps became infected and they died" (Freeman 1989: 261; see also Jade Ngoc Quang Huynh 1994 for an account of reeducation camps).

After they were released, the former prisoners, many of whom had been broken physically and mentally, had to report to local authorities, who kept a watch on them. One man whom I interviewed was released early from the camps because he had lost a leg during the war, but for the next fifteen years he was kept under house arrest in his village. Others were denied employment and had to survive under the most difficult of circumstances. Since the late 1980s, under the Humanitarian Operation program mentioned in Chapter 1, more than 23,000 former political prisoners and their immediate families have been allowed to emigrate to the United States.

Even for those who were not prisoners, life was extremely harsh. In 1975, the Communists immediately abolished the old currency, destroying its value and instantly impoverishing millions of people. The Communists forced the relocation of tens of thousands of urban people to the countryside, where they were made to cultivate often inhospitable lands under dreadful living conditions. One woman showed me her swollen, crippled hands with which she had been forced to dig holes for sugar cane. The aim, never realized, was to relocate three million people to new economic areas and another ten million for other projects. In 1978, all major businesses and industries in the South were nationalized and goods were confiscated. Shortly after, a new currency was issued, again disrupting and impoverishing the population. The forced exchange of currency occurred three times, each time with a small maximum cap of money that a person could receive back. Attempts were made to collectivize agriculture and to institute production quotas. These succeeded in some areas but failed, for example, in the Mekong delta.

Many of these attempted economic reforms met with passive resistance and attempts at evasion, including flight from the area. Because of shortages of consumer goods, black market operations increased, as did the corruption of officials. In 1978 and 1979, grain harvests were poor and people throughout the country went hungry. Meanwhile, Vietnam became involved in a brief but bloody border war with China and a war and ten-year military occupation of Cambodia. In Vietnam today, one sees countless young men missing one or more limbs, not from the earlier war of the North and the South, but from the Cambodian campaign. The wars with

China and Cambodia further drained Vietnam's already scarce resources, causing unemployment and poverty, massive food shortages, and numerous health crises, including extensive malnutrition, which as late as the 1990s, afflicted over 40 percent of Vietnam's children (Socialist Republic of Vietnam 1992: 42).

In addition, the government intruded deeply into the private lives of its citizens. One man told me how he was forced to spy on his neighbors and submit secret reports on them. "I had to comply. I saw what they did to people in my company who did not do what they want; they sent them to jail. I described my neighbors doing chores at home or playing ping pong, nothing harmful. I hated doing these reports. Because I had been educated abroad and spoke English well, I knew I was regarded as a discredited element. I knew I had to get out of the country, to escape or die trying."

A Buddhist nun explained the climate of fear under which people lived. "Whenever people visited me, they complained about the Communist invasion of their privacy. They were especially upset that nobody could trust anybody, for Communist agents were everywhere in disguise.... If they saw you talking to another person, they would immediately separate you and ask you both to write on a piece of paper what topic you had discussed., and turn you in if your reports were in disagreement....Parents dared not talk to their own children, for the next day the children might involuntarily reveal something to their friends at school. Even husbands and wives became wary of one another" (Freeman 1989: 274).

In his powerful account of the first years under Communist control, *After Saigon Fell*, Nguyen Long, who subsequently escaped as a boat person with his family, discusses daily life under the Communists, including shortages of fuel and food as well as restrictions on individual movement. To travel to another town, a person had to acquire a travel permit or he or she would be arrested on the trip. Buying a bus ticket was complicated and expensive; it involved standing in line for hours if not days, buying black market tickets, and paying extra for packages to be carried on the bus. The police intimidated travelers with their inspections of packages. In addition, travelers had to bring food with them; the families they visited did not have extra food to offer to a guest, they only had what was rationed to them for their own needs (Nguyen Long 1981: 55-80).

Many refugees who fled Vietnam did so, not primarily because of the economic hardships, but because their freedoms had been taken away from them. Intimidation by the police and other officials, while lessened, remains to this day, and continues to be a source of frustration and anger for many people. Disillusion with Communist Vietnam has come not only from the defeated South Vietnamese, but from the victors as well. A widely acclaimed Viet Cong hero confided to me, "I fought against the French and we won; I fought against the Americans and we won. I am proud of my achievements. I was on the right side. I believe in Socialism. But what I've seen after the war, breaks my heart. The society we have now is not what I fought and risked my life for during all those years."

Fearful of expressing opposition openly, writers and film makers have frequently resorted to indirect criticism. An example is the 1987 film *Chuyen Tu Te* or *The Story of How to Behave*, directed by Tran Van Thuy, which makes guarded references to inequalities in the country. Communist officials, the servants of the country, ride in limousines; the people whom they serve push into a crowded bus, and former war heroes are shown destitute on the streets. Originally commissioned by the Vietnamese government, apparently to demonstrate its openness to criticism, it was banned from public viewing after being released (Freeman and Nguyen 1991: 479-481).

In the 1990s, criticism has grown more open. *The Sorrow of War*, a graphic and controversial novel by North Vietnamese Army veteran Bao Ninh, depicts his disillusion with war, his sense of betrayal for the ways the returning soldiers were abandoned, and his anger because the victory for which they fought turned out to be hollow. Bao Ninh himself was one of ten survivors out of five hundred of the Glorious 27th Youth Brigade. In his novel, a soldier says, "In all my time as a soldier, I've yet to see anything honorable." After the war, a resident of Hanoi says, "The victory we got was a victory for morons. Call that civilization and progress? Garbage!" (Bao Ninh 1993: 18, 143).

Throughout Vietnam today, one hears people saying privately, "The Communists just talk, they cannot accomplish anything." As William Duiker explains: "In part, this is a natural consequence of the sense of disillusionment experienced by many Vietnamese after two decades of political and economic malaise. But it also represents the beginning of an effort to reevaluate the trajectory of the Vietnamese revolution and to judge it in terms of its real accomplishments and failures rather than in the heroic terms ascribed to it by the ruling Communist Party" (1995b: 270-271).

In late 1986, the Sixth Congress of the Communist Party approved a thoroughgoing reform of their centrally planned system in reaction to shortages of rice, which caused inflation up to 400 percent, a declining standard of living, limited export growth, large budget deficits, and several other crises. The reforms also paralleled changes occurring in the former Soviet Union, Vietnam's principal economic benefactor at that time. Referred to as Renovation, the reforms, while primarily economic, also called for a gradual liberalization of the Communist Party, national assembly, and the press. Among the dramatic and risky policy changes approved was one encouraging foreign direct investment and, as Myo Thant and Richard Vokes note, "a reliance on or acceptance of the private sector as the engine of economic growth." They conclude, "The economic progress achieved in Vietnam since the inception of the post-1986 reform measures has been extensive by any measure. The progress is all the more remarkable since the reform measures were carried out almost entirely without external funding and assistance and implemented even while major fundamental changes in external economic relations were taking place" (Myo Thant and Vokes 1993: 241).

Other momentous changes have occurred: attempts to improve international relations, especially with Vietnam's immediate neighbors, the withdrawal from Cambodia after ten years of occupation, the encouragement of overseas Vietnamese to return and help rebuild the country, and the improvement of relations with the United States, which in 1994 lifted its economic embargo of Vietnam and in 1995 reestablished diplomatic relations with Vietnam. American companies are doing business in Vietnam, as are thousands of overseas Vietnamese, many of whom are U.S. citizens. There are educational and cultural exchanges between the United States and Vietnam. Americans, once seen by Vietnamese Communists as the enemy, are now welcomed when they visit Vietnam.

Because refugees and immigrants from Vietnam are recent arrivals in the United States, their ties to their homeland remain strong. Nearly all still have relatives in Vietnam; many have kept in touch with these relatives over the years, sending them money and goods, and more recently visiting them. As Vietnam continues to open its doors to outsiders, especially Americans, Vietnam will remain an important part of the lives of many Vietnamese Americans.

At the same time, Vietnamese Americans have changed in numerous ways and are no longer entirely like their relatives in Vietnam. Many Vietnamese refugees and immigrants, and, even more, their children born in America, have adopted American behaviors and values which are in startling contrast to old-country Vietnamese ways. This book explores how Vietnamese Americans have integrated these two different life styles and how they themselves think about the changes that have occurred in their lives. However, before turning to this question, we must consider one additional formative influence in their lives, their journey as refugees and immigrants to the United States.

3

Seeking Freedom

The journey to America is one of the formative experiences affecting how the Vietnamese have adjusted in the United States. One writer has suggested that the agony and ordeal of escape "was like high-altitude training for athletes" because those who survived have a strong desire to make the most of their escape (Weiss 1994: 36). But many did not survive, and among those who did, thousands carry crippling memories of savage treatment in Vietnam, on their escapes, and in refugee camps.

The flight of Vietnamese asylum seekers is often characterized as a series of "waves:" first, those who left when Saigon fell in 1975; second, ethnic Chinese who left in 1978 and 1979; third, a large number who escaped by boat or overland between 1978 and 1982; fourth, intermittent smaller movements of asylum seekers between 1983 and 1989. Finally, the fifth wave includes those who arrived in countries of first asylum after March 14, 1989 (June 6, 1988 for Hong Kong). After these dates, new arrivals had to be evaluated for refugee status under a new international agreement called the Comprehensive Plan of Action. Those given refugee status were entitled to be considered for resettlement in countries such as the United States; those denied refugee status were told they had to return to Vietnam. In addition to these five waves of refugees, many of whom came from refugee camps, thousands of Vietnamese have come directly from

Vietnam to America, not as refugees, but as legal immigrants, often sponsored by close relatives. Each of these groups have had significantly different experiences, both of migration and of adjustments to America.

THE FIRST WAVE: 1975

Prior to the fall of Saigon in 1975, only a small number of Vietnamese had immigrated to the United States. In the 1950s, the immigrants, numbering a little over 200, were mostly university students; in the 1960s, Vietnamese immigrants increased to a little over 3,000, including some war brides, a reflection of America's involvement in the Vietnam war. Between 1970 and 1974, the number jumped to over 14,500. In all, before the end of the war the total number of Vietnamese in America was just over 18,000 (Rumbaut 1995: 240-241).

The rapid military collapse of South Vietnam in the Spring of 1975 surprised the North Vietnamese, the South Vietnamese, and the American governments. Only in late April, 1975, as the collapse of South Vietnam became certain, did the Americans begin a belated emergency airlift to evacuate American military and diplomatic personnel, along with some at-risk Vietnamese: members of the South Vietnamese army and government, and those who had worked for the Americans. Officials in Washington had been reluctant to bring out the Vietnamese, first because it might cause a panic among others in Vietnam, and second because of a recession in the United States, anti-immigrant sentiment, and hostility to the Vietnam war. Plans for the evacuation were made secretly by many lower level-American State Department and military personnel who had been on tours of duty in Vietnam and who believed that the United States had a moral obligation to help their Vietnamese allies. Had it not been for their efforts, many more Vietnamese would have been abandoned (Kelly 1979: 11-23; Butler 1985; Snepp 1978: 566).

As it was, tens of thousands of Vietnamese with legitimate authorization for evacuation were left behind, while others who were not targeted for evacuation escaped in the turmoil and panic of the final days and hours. Some ten to fifteen thousands escaped in the ten days before the collapse of South Vietnam; another eighty-six thousand Vietnamese and Americans were brought out in the last few days of April. In those days and the two weeks following the fall of Saigon, another forty to sixty thousand Vietnamese made their way in small boats to the American Seventh Fleet or to Vietnamese navy ships in the South China Sea; others escaped to Hong Kong or Thailand. Of the people who left Vietnam at that time about 130,000 were resettled in the United States, while another 60,000 refugees were held in refugee camps in Hong Kong or Thailand (Liu 1979: 13-14; Kelly 1979: 36).

Mr. Le Van Hieu, now a computer specialist in an electronics firm in the San Francisco Bay area, recalls his final days in Vietnam, when he was 13 years old. "On the night of April 29, 1975, my life in Vietnam ended. I escaped in a small tugboat containing 55 people, 37 of whom were relatives, including my parents, my younger sister, and my three younger brothers. My father's younger brother, who was in the South Vietnamese navy, had outfitted the boat with food, water, and weapons. My father did not want to leave, even though he had spent four years in the USA and had been in the army and the government of South Vietnam. He only did so because his parents refused to leave unless he went with them. At first, I didn't think much about leaving. Then, around 11:00 A.M. the next morning, we heard over the radio that South Vietnam had fallen to the Communists. Then I realized I was not going to return. A sad feeling sank in. I felt empty. My family had fled the Communists in the North in 1954. Now we were fleeing again. My family was picked up at sea and taken to Subic Bay in the Philippines, then to Wake Island for two or three months, then to Camp Pendleton in California. It was great for kids: no school, just eating and playing. For the adults, especially the women, it was very hard. They had lost everything, and now they worried what the future would bring."

MASS EXODUS OF ETHNIC CHINESE AND THE INTERNATIONAL RESPONSE: 1978-1982

In 1968, during the Tet Offensive, the Communists briefly occupied the central Vietnamese city of Hue. During that time, they rounded up and shot, clubbed, and buried alive some 3,000 residents—army officers as well as civilians and their families—suspected of being linked to the South Vietnamese government. Because of this massacre, many South Vietnamese feared what would happen when the Communists won in 1975, and the American press predicted a bloodbath. This contributed to the panic of the first wave refugees as they sought to escape.

The bloodbath did not occur, and at first few people tried to escape. In 1975, once the first wave refugees had left, only 378 people fled Vietnam and landed in countries of first asylum. But as the impact of gradual social transformations were felt, including the persecution of individuals and suppression of freedoms, more fled. In 1976, the number of escapees jumped to 5,247; in 1977, 15,690 people escaped. In 1978 and 1979, the numbers skyrocketed to 85,213 and 185, 826 respectively: between May 1975 and July 31, 1979, 292,315 Vietnamese successfully escaped by boat. This was but a fraction of the total number of 1.7 million displaced persons who in four years had fled from persecution not only in Vietnam, but in the neighboring countries of Cambodia and Laos (Grant 1979: 215-217; Wain 1981: 79-80).

In the past 400 years, sizable Chinese communities developed in Vietnam. The Chinese played an important role in urban business, controlling markets such as rice and pepper. (Whitmore 1985: 59-68). Between 1978 and 1980, the majority of the hundreds of thousands of boat people leaving Vietnam were ethnic Chinese, victims of anti-Chinese sentiment fueled by a border clash with China in 1979, and the decision by Hanoi in the same year to nationalize businesses in the South (Whitmore 1985: 59-68; Zolberg, Suhrke, and Aguayo 1989: 164). The refugees brought with them reports of how their wealth had been confiscated by authorities before they were allowed to leave. In some cases, Vietnamese officials connived to engineer the departure of the ethnic Chinese in return for kickbacks. Over 200,000 ethnic chinese were resettled in the United States as refugees from Vietnam, though many later identified themselves for the U.S. Census as Chinese, not Vietnamese (Das and Sacerdoti 1978: 10-11; Freeman 1989: 410; Weintraub 1978: 8-10; Wain 1981: 15-35).

The voyages of the Vietnamese boat people fleeing from persecution were as remarkable as they were often tragic. One of the greatest feats of navigation ever recorded was that of a Vietnamese fishing boat containing 56 people which landed in Australia after a journey of some 5,000 miles (Grant 1979: 16-19).

A former schoolteacher told me how he escaped from central Vietnam in 1976. Within two months of the Communist victory in 1975, Mr. Phuong Hoang decided that he had to leave. He prepared for almost one year. He and a friend bought a boat, taught themselves how to navigate with a small Japanese compass and by looking at the stars, bought a fishing permit, and hid supplies on a small island off the coast. They and their families escaped. Near Manila, as their boat was sinking in a storm, an Italian freighter rescued them and brought them to Italy. A refugee agency resettled them in America. He says, "Looking back on it now, our sea voyage, with only a toy compass to guide us, was very dangerous. Still, it would have been better to die at sea than live another day under Communist rule" (Freeman 1989: 310-312).

Others were not so fortunate. Thousands of people failed in their attempts to escape, missing rendezvous, being cheated by people who claimed to be organizing escapes, and being caught by security forces while trying to flee Vietnam. Since, according to Vietnamese law, leaving the country without permission was a crime, those who were caught were placed in jail, women and children in one room, the men in another.

Despite failures, refugees made repeated attempts to escape. If, finally, they succeeded in eluding the shore guards and coastal patrols, they still faced the dangerous storms and swirling tides of the South China sea. Beyond that, the waters around Thailand and Malaysia were infested with pirates who often worked in teams of boats to rape, pillage, and murder their hapless victims. At least ten percent of the asylum seekers lost their lives while trying to escape, though some estimates are much higher; by 1987 the estimate was at least 100,000 (Richardson 1979: 34; Rumbaut 1995: 238). Of the surviving boats, one out of three was stopped by pirates, who robbed their victims, and of those that were stopped, one out of three were subjected additionally to rape and murder. Not only Thai pirates, but Vietnamese patrols killed wantonly (Das 1978: 13; Nhat Tien, Duong Phuc, Vu Thanh Thuy 1981; Richardson 1979: 34; Freeman 1989: 325-335).

As hundreds of thousands of refugees fled Vietnam, Laos, and Cambodia, neighboring countries in Southeast Asia and Hong Kong found themselves unable or unwilling to absorb the stream of refugees that threatened to overwhelm them. Although China and Japan had done so, none of the Southeast Asian countries had signed the 1951 United Nations Convention Relating to the Status of Refugees and its 1967 Protocol, which provided guidelines for the protection of asylum seekers. Of particular importance was the principle that people should not be returned against their will to a place where they feared persecution (Wain 1981: 31-32; Muntarbhorn 1992: 31, 83, 163-191).

Countries such as Thailand and Malaysia threatened to refuse to allow the boat people to land, claiming that the Indochina conflict that had produced these asylum seekers was not of their making, and that they were already housing refugees with no guarantee that subsequently the refugees would be resettled elsewhere. In a number of well publicized cases, Vietnamese refugee boats attempting to land in Thailand and Malaysia were towed back out to sea. In Malaysia, some 40,000 Vietnamese were pushed back, though some simply landed further along the coast. While announcing a hard line, in practice Thailand and Malaysia allowed some boats to land and placed the new arrivals in temporary camps.

The United Nations organization that is committed to the protection of refugees is the office of the United Nations High Commissioner for Refugees (UNHCR). Although slow to respond at first to the Indochinese refugee crisis, in 1979 the UNHCR negotiated with Vietnam the Orderly Departure

Program (ODP), which would allow qualified persons to be resettled directly from Vietnam to countries such as the United States and Canada. People coming into the United States under the ODP were processed either as refugees under the Refugee Act of 1980 or as immigrants under the Immigrant and Nationality Act. The Refugee Act of 1980 was passed to provide a means of regulating admissions into the United States. It widened the notion of refugee to include, not only those fleeing Communism, but asylum seekers from other oppressive regimes (Kennedy: 1981: 143). The definition of refugee was similar to that developed by the United Nations in 1951, which defined a refugee as a person who was unable or unwilling to return to or be put under the protection of the country in which they last habitually resided, "because of persecution or a well-founded fear of persecution on account of race, religion, nationality, membership in a particular social group, or political opinion" (Rutledge 1992: 36; Zolberg, Suhrke, and Aguayo 1989: 25).

Under the ODP, Vietnamese could enter the United States if they had close relatives living in the United States who applied to bring them over: spouses, sons, daughters, parents, grandparents, and unmarried grandchildren. Others who qualified were those who had been employed by Americans or American companies in Vietnam, or officials, soldiers, and their close relatives who had been associated with the United States. Finally, those who had other ties to America might qualify, ranging from students who had studied in the United States, to Amerasians, that is, people whose mothers were Vietnamese and fathers were American citizens. In December, 1987, the U.S. Congress passed the Amerasian Homecoming Act, which allowed 40,000 Amerasians and their relatives to come to America through 1994.

The ODP was a great improvement over the costly and dangerous illegal departures of the boat people. In theory it allowed people to leave Vietnam safely and legally. But as Zolberg, Suhrke, and Aguayo point out, at first the beneficiaries were not classical refugees, those whose lives and well-being were threatened by Vietnamese authorities. Vietnam would not allow such people to leave, feeling that they might mobilize in exile against Vietnam. Political prisoners were excluded from the ODP until 1984, when the USA and Vietnam agreed to allow 10,000 former reeducation camp prisoners to emigrate to America. Even then, Vietnam only slowly released these people over several years. Most of the early ODP arrivals were people brought in under the principle of family reunion (Zolberg, Suhrke, and Aguayo 1989: 167). In 1988, the US State Department pledged to secure the release and resettlement of the remaining 85,000 reeducation camp prisoners who had been incarcerated for at least three years; most of them had been brought to America by 1995.

The process of the ODP was bureaucratic and lengthy. The United States or other countries of resettlement had to be willing to accept a particular person and Vietnam had to be willing to let that person go. In its early years, Vietnam and the United States disagreed about who should be allowed to leave. The United States hoped to bring in persons who qualified under the ODP criteria. Vietnam used the ODP to get rid of those whom they considered undesirable, including Amerasians as well as ethnic Chinese who did not meet ODP qualifications. Vietnamese officials refused or delayed the release of many people considered eligible by the United States (Lee 1979: 30).

Although it was denied by Hanoi, applying for ODP made Vietnamese vulnerable to the harassment of officials, who could deny educational or employment opportunities to an applicant's family while holding up applications until they received payoffs. At best, the ODP took years, with the result that many qualified people turned again to illegal boat departures. In 1991, I met a woman, 75 years old, the oldest boat person in the Philippine refugee camp of Palawan. She was in line for the ODP, since her daughter was a permanent resident in the United States. After several years of waiting, she grew impatient, hopped on a boat, and escaped. She was not allowed to resettle from the Philippines; she had to return to Vietnam and leave from there.

LIFE IN THE CAMPS

After surviving perilous journeys, virtually all boat people were placed in primitive and crowded refugee camps in countries of first asylum, where they had to remain for the six months to a year it would take to resettle them. In July, 1978, Pulau Bidong was an uninhabited island 18 miles off the coast of peninsular Malaysia. Five months later, it was "swarming with 25,000 Vietnamese waiting for the outside world to determine their future." Despite severe crowding, insufficient materials to build temporary shelters, fears of contamination of the wells, the nearly total absence of medicine, and a food ration for each refugee of only one half pint of rice per day and one tin of sardines every five days, the Vietnamese had organized the camp to make the best use of human and material resources. They developed an organization that allocated responsibilities for "supplies, security, construction, information and culture, social welfare (including health, water supply, and sanitation), interpreters, and administration" (Das and Sacerdoti 1978: 10-11).

By 1979, as refugees continued to pour in, Pilau Bidong became, "a dangerously congested slum...a shantytown with a population of 42,000 confined to a living area of less than one square kilometer." Shanties, some three stories high, were constructed of timber beams with walls of cardboard, tin, or timber, with roofs of blue plastic sheeting or waterproof sugar sacks. "The beach was fouled with heaps of rubbish rotting in the heat and humidity...flies swarmed everywhere and the stench of human excrement was oppressive." Wells were polluted or dry, and the acute shortage of water led to long lines of people waiting to get a few drops. Tempers flared and fights were frequent. People had nothing to do but sit (Grant 1979: 75-76; Freeman 1989: 317).

Some camps were far more brutal. Of Sikhiu, a camp in central Thailand, one youth now in America said, "For minor infractions, the guards would string us up by our thumbs and leave us hanging until we passed out. To make sure we were unconscious, they would burn us with lighted cigarettes" (see also Freeman 1989: 346-347).

The most brutal of the camps were on the tense, unsettled border of Thailand and Cambodia. Mrs. Do Thanh Hue, a Vietnamese refugee now living in California, described to me her life in one of those border camps, known as Site 2. "Vietnamese troops occupying Cambodia used to fire at us; in some months, shelling went on continuously, day after day. It was an indescribable horror; we would hear the screams and cries of the wounded; bodies were everywhere, and blood was all over the road. We were terrified; there was no place to hide. Our family simply huddled together, embraced one another, and cried. Cambodian bandits, in groups of 70 to 80, would attack the camp at night. But the greatest danger for us came from the Thai camp guards. They killed, raped, and beat people whenever they wanted. Almost every youngster was hit on the head with rifles two or three times. One time, three Vietnamese youths were talking with a Laotian girl. The guards grabbed the boys, pulled out knives, and sliced up and down their arms until blood flowed freely. They poured vinegar on the wounds to cause the young men great pain. Then they buried the three of them alive. I saw that. And I was there when they stopped a Cambodian woman from selling fried bananas in the market. She was not permitted to do that, so the guards took the boiling oil from her pan and poured it on her head. Her two eyes blew up and she died instantly, right in front of her two small children....With the never-ending hunger, the shelling, the Cambodian bandits, the Thai guards, the continuous fear of death and torture at any moment, the dirt, the lack of privacy, the exhaustion, the disease, and the uncertainty of what was to happen to us,...we were always in a panic."(Freeman and Nguyen: in press)

COMPASSION FATIGUE AND THE COMPREHENSIVE PLAN OF ACTION: 1989

In the late 1970s and early 1980s, as hundreds of thousands of Vietnamese fled their homeland, the world opened its doors, though at first reluctantly, to resettle them as refugees. However, by 1989, 160,000 asylum seekers, many of them from North Vietnam, were in Southeast Asian camps. But now world sentiment had reversed. Countries both of first asylum and of final resettlement were less willing to accept the new boat people as refugees; instead, they referred to them as economic migrants. Officials in these countries talked of compassion fatigue and expressed concerns about how to stem the continuous flow of boat people.

In 1989, to discourage continued escapes from Vietnam by asylum seekers, the UNHCR convened a multinational conference in Geneva. Seventy-eight nations signed and adopted a Comprehensive Plan of Action (CPA), one of the provisions of which was the designation of March 14, 1989 (June 6 1988 for Hong Kong) as the cutoff date for asylum seekers. Persons arriving in countries of first asylum before that date were automatically accepted as refugees. Representatives of the countries of resettlement interviewed them to determine whether or not to admit them. In general, those who had already had relatives in the United States or who could prove that they had been involved with the American presence in Vietnam were more easily admitted to the United States. By contrast, those arriving after the cutoff date had to prove they qualified for refugee status by going through a screening process. Those declared refugees qualified to be resettled. Those screened out were told to repatriate or return to their country of origin. They would not be forcibly sent back to Vietnam because that violated international rules protecting asylum seekers, and because Vietnam would not accept anyone who refused to return voluntarily.

Children under the age of 16 who, for one reason or another, had arrived in refugee camps without a parent, were evaluated by a Special Committee to determine if resettlement or repatriation was in their best interests. The Committee consisted of immigration officials of the country of first asylum, aided by a UNHCR official and an expert on children.

Since March, 1989, over 200,000 asylum seekers arrived in refugee camps. Some 75-80 percent of these post-CPA asylum seekers were screened out and denied refugee status. This happened despite protests from charitable and human rights organizations throughout the world that the screening process was flawed and strongly biased against asylum seekers, and that, in several countries, refugee status was bought for sexual favors or money. Because of this, over 45,000 screened-out asylum seekers had refused to repatriate to Vietnam by

March 1995. To resolve this situation, the international community, including the UNHCR and Vietnam, agreed to repatriate screened-out asylum seekers against their will, with the expectation that all camps would close by 1996, and the Vietnamese boat people saga, which began in 1975, would come to an end. Under different rules, the forcible repatriation of unaccompanied minors began at the end of June 1993. Many of the camps were expected to close by the end of 1995.

The Comprehensive Plan of Action has been hailed as a political success, in that, with rare exceptions, people no longer attempt to escape from Vietnam. But from the point of view of the asylum seekers, especially the children who make up one half of the population of the camps, it has been a human disaster. For the several thousand who have subsequently resettled in the United States, their long stay of four to five years in these camps has made their adjustments in America all the more difficult.

While experiencing all of the horrors of the camps, children faced additional problems. They often received little or no education (violating the International Convention on the Rights of the Child), had nothing to do, and had little parental guidance or control. Even if they had relatives with them, these adults, as fellow detainees, had limited authority. Unaccompanied minors were particularly lonely and depressed. Particularly harmful to them was the length of time that they stayed in the camp. Earlier boat people remained only for six months to one year. Post-CPA asylum seekers, including children, were locked away for two to five years or more as their cases for refugee status were heard and sometimes appealed. Children were also coerced and intimidated into participating in political demonstrations. They witnessed riots, suicides by stabbing or burning, and mass protests in which prisoners slashed their bellies with homemade weapons (Freeman and Nguyen n.d.).

The voices of the children reveal despair, cynicism, and hope. One such voice is that of Do Phuong Vi, a 17 year old girl now struggling in an American high school. She recalls the camps as places of "riots and killing, boredom and loneliness." Another girl, 14, said to me, "I am afraid, but I do not know how to deal with my fear." A child told an American volunteer working in the Philippines, "I want to kill myself, but my religion says it is wrong. So I pray that I die in my sleep."

THE TIMING OF ARRIVAL IN AMERICA

The experience of those who have come to America since 1989 is not at all like that of the first wave refugees or the boat people of previous years. First wave refugees arrived at a time when the American and world economic situation was better, and refugee programs included three years of financial assistance, English instruction, and job training. As the next chapter shows, many of these people and their children have achieved striking successes in school, jobs, and in adjusting to American ways. Despite traumatic experiences in escaping and in enduring up to one year in refugee camps, many of the earlier boat people have also succeeded. Some say that the very hardship and dangers they encountered made their determination to succeed all the stronger.

The post-CPA arrivals, both immigrants coming directly from Vietnam and boat people given refugee status, have had different experiences and have found a different America. The new arrivals endured years of abuse and hardship in post-war Vietnam. Some are former reeducation camp prisoners who suffered years of starvation and mistreatment. Others spent years in New Economic Zones in Vietnam doing hard physical labor. Still others have had to eke out a living on the margins of Vietnamese society, doing whatever was necessary to survive. In the camps, they stagnated while becoming dependent on camp authorities for food or on money sent by relatives in the United States.

In America, their skills rarely prepare them for work. With layoffs and economic problems in the United States in the middle 1990s, jobs are hard to get and hold. Refugee assistance, English instruction, and job-training programs have been drastically cut. The newly arrived Vietnamese also face rising anti-immigrant sentiment. In this environment, their expectations of what the United States has to offer regarding wealth, jobs, and even support by their relatives are often unrealistic.

For the refugee camp children who have recently come to the United States, the situation is even worse; the camps have thoroughly disrupted their childhood and shattered their lives. Because of their long stay in the camps, they face difficulties for which they need special counseling and guidance. They are several years behind in school and have a hard time catching up. They find it difficult to cope with a new language and customs while being place in an unfamiliar school setting. Because of their experiences of abuse in the camps, they are frequently disillusioned, resentful, and distrustful of authority. After years of running wild in the camps with little or no parental guidance or discipline, they are hard to control; they do not adjust easily in traditional family settings. They have little in common with Vietnamese-American children who were born in the United States or who came here several years ago.

This chapter has introduced two points that are developed further in this book. The first is that the post-CPA refugees and immigrants are having a more difficult time than their predecessors. The timing of their leaving Vietnam and arrival in the United States is a major factor in how the Vietnamese adjust to America. As the Vietnamese say, "The buffalo that arrives late to the river drinks the muddy water."

The second point is that the cultures, lives, and identities of Vietnamese refugees and immigrants (and other people too) are powerfully influenced by national and international events, past and present, and by global economic and political forces. Vietnamese identity and character have been forged over the centuries by their contact with South and Southeast Asian cultures and China, and more recently with France and the United States. The conflicts that have flared in Vietnam over the past 150 years owe much to European colonialism and to the cold war conflicts between the major powers. The mass migrations of Vietnamese out of their homeland, and the various ways in which they have been defined, received, or rejected by other countries, are understandable only in this wider global context. Without these global forces and events, the Vietnamese would not be in America, redefining themselves and their culture in new ways on a foreign soil.

4

Resettlement and Employment: Overcoming Adversity

At the time of the fall of Saigon, public opinion polls showed that a majority of Americans, 54 percent, were opposed to letting Vietnamese refugees come to live in the United States; only 36 percent were in favor. Not only ordinary citizens, but some officials expressed harsh views. Governor Brown of California, who initially opposed the resettlement of any Vietnamese refugees in his state, remarked, "We can't be looking five thousand miles away and at the same time neglecting people who are living here." Senator McGovern, well known for his anti-Vietnam war views, said, "Ninety percent of the Vietnamese refugees would be better off going back to their own land" (Engelmann 1995: 5; Liu 1979: 63; Hein 1993: 34). Sociologist William Liu claims that the initial negative reaction against the refugees "was bred in an atmosphere of rumors, economic self-interest, guilt reactions, and racism."

However, a number of influential elected officials, newspaper editors, and prominent Americans, including AFL-CIO President George Meany, strongly advocated bringing in the Vietnamese on humanitarian grounds. They felt a sense of guilt and responsibility for what had happened in Vietnam, Laos, and Cambodia, as well as obligation to some of its victims. Supporters of this view tended to be those with higher incomes and education, and they included many who had opposed the war.

In April 1975, an Interagency Task Force on Indochinese Refugees composed of twelve federal agencies was established to oversee the resettlement of the refugees in America over a period of two years. President Ford announced that he would use his parole power, or authority to grant refugee status, to admit 130,000 people from Indochina. Despite negative remarks made by some legislators, Congress voted overwhelmingly in May, 1975 to approve $405 million in aid for refugee resettlement, and President Ford signed the bill into law ten days later. By that time, the rescue operation had taken place, and some refugees were already in the United States, while others were being processed in temporary camps such as at Guam. In comparison with the staggering cost of the Vietnam war, $165 billion, the amount allocated for the refugees was minuscule, and it was well under the $583 million that had been used to resettle the Cubans, almost half of whom came as immigrants.

While sponsors were being found, the refugees were housed temporarily at one of four military bases: Camp Pendleton, California, Fort Chaffee, Arkansas, Fort Indian Town Gap, Pennsylvania, and Eglin Air Force Base, Florida. Various agencies making up the Interagency Task Force were assigned specific duties: resettling the refugees throughout the United States, and giving them English language instruction, vocational training, medical care, psychological counseling, and cultural orientation to help them adjust. Federal funds were used to reimburse all state and local expenditures for refugees as a way of alleviating concerns that resettlement would be an economic burden on local communities. To further lessen the impact of the Vietnamese on local schools, health services, employment, and welfare, the Interagency Task Force recommended that the refugees be dispersed throughout the United States (Hein 1993: 24-30; Kelly 1977: 64; Kennedy 1981: 143; Liu 1979: 66-69; Loescher and Scanlon 1986: 119; Reimers 1992: 178-179).

THE REFUGEE CAMPS IN AMERICA

The U.S. government originally intended to evacuate only those few thousand Vietnamese employed in Vietnam by Americans and the dependents of American citizens. These people were expected to adjust quickly and easily to American society. But with the unanticipated rapid collapse of South Vietnam, and the chaotic, unplanned mass exodus of the Vietnamese, many were not those whom the Americans expected to evacuate. Many former elites did not have immediately marketable skills in America, and well over 60 percent spoke no English. The four refugee camps in America were where the refugees began to learn to adjust to life in the United States.

William Liu, who studied refugees in Camp Pendleton, concludes that considerable effort was made to help the new arrivals, though he believes that inadequate attention was given to mental health needs, the cultural values of the refugees, and problems that might occur in resettlement, including the breakup and dispersal of extended families. In her discussion of problems at Fort Indian Town Gap, Gail Kelly agrees with Liu that the most traumatic policy was the breaking apart of extended families into nuclear families so that they could be dispersed and resettled with different sponsors (Liu 1979: 114-118; Kelly 1977: 91-127). However, many refugees recall their days in the military bases with nostalgia. At a reunion at Camp Pendleton, twenty years after its opening, former refugees, now successful middle class Americans, reminisced and showed their American-born children how the refugees got their start. Their memories were bittersweet, triggering recollections of the loss of their native country, but they also came "with gratitude for the Marines and their new homeland" (Tran 1995: 24A; see also Engelmann 1995: 1, 4-5C).

SPONSORS AND THE REACTIONS OF AMERICAN COMMUNITIES

Refugees could leave the camp only if they had enough money to be financially self-supporting ($4000 per family member), wished to return to Vietnam, could be resettled in another country, or could find an American individual or group that would sponsor them. Ninety-nine percent of the Vietnamese opted for the fourth choice. In many instances, sponsorship was arranged through organizations known as voluntary agencies. Many of them, such as the United States Catholic Conference, Lutheran Social Services, and the International Rescue Committee, had resettled earlier immigrants who had come to America. A sponsor was expected to find food, clothing, and shelter for the refugees until they became self-supporting. They were also expected to help the refugees in adjusting to America: enrolling their children in school, helping them find employment, and teaching them American customs. At first, they were also expected to take on the responsibility of health care, except for unemployed refugees who received Medicare. For all of this, a sponsor received $500; it has been estimated that the actual expenses were close to $6,000, and that was assuming that the Vietnamese could pay for their own food after one week and their own rent after one month.

Because the financial obligations were so great, it was sometimes difficult to find American families who were willing or able to become sponsors; but some did, generously giving their money, time, and effort to help the Vietnamese. Many volunteer workers in the camps also ended up sponsoring families. The voluntary agencies, as well as local community organizations, found individuals, churches, and companies to sponsor the refugees. Despite the dangers of exploitation, sponsorship by an employer was widely encouraged, because it led to economic self sufficiency for the refugees. By the end of 1975, 129,792 Vietnamese had been resettled, around 50 percent by the United States Catholic Conference and around 15 percent by the International Rescue Committee (Englelmann 1995: 1,4-5C; Kelly 1977: 129-166).

While the Vietnamese reported some difficulties with sponsors (see Kelly 1977), many refugees recall with gratitude and affection the generous treatment of their American sponsors. A former high military officer, Colonel Tran Dinh Bui, remembers how he, his wife, and their eight children, all Buddhists, were welcomed and taken care of by church-

based sponsors in a small Alabama town. Now a social worker on the West Coast, Colonel Bui has kept in touch with the
people of that town and plans to visit them again.

Mrs. That, whose family was initially resettled in a small
town in Arkansas, recalls that her sponsors treated her family, "just like sisters and brothers," inviting them to stay in
their house for two months and giving them meals. Then her
sponsors found a nearby townhouse for her family to rent at
a low price because it was owned by a member of the sponsor's church. The people of the church gave them pots and
dishes, beds, blankets and sheets, a washing machine, an
electric stove and a refrigerator. All of their material needs
were met. Members of the church hired her children to work.
Mrs. That remarked, "The Vietnamese people would never
have done for complete strangers what they did for us. It was
precious." Her husband changed his name to an American
name and became a Christian. In their house, a cross now
hangs in place of an ancestral family shrine. I asked him
about this, and he said, "No one ever tried to change my beliefs, but I'm in America now; I did this out of gratitude for
our sponsors." By contrast, some refugees reported to me that
their sponsors exerted pressure on them to convert.

Despite the generosity they had received, after one year
Mrs. That and her family decided to leave the sponsors' town,
where they were the only Vietnamese family, joining thousands of other Vietnamese who became secondary migrants.
Upon hearing the news, the sponsor burst into tears. "She
begged us not to leave. The church people also tried to per-
suade us to stay. In the meantime, our children [who had already moved to California] hurried us up to move, so we told
our sponsor our decision, and they had to accept....I regret
that we moved" (Freeman 1989: 369-371).

Not all communities welcomed the refugees. The sudden
arrival of the Vietnamese in the United States occurred during a time of rising anti-immigrant sentiment. The 1965 Immigration Act had opened up immigration to larger numbers of
people from Asia, Latin America, and the Caribbean. By 1977,
these groups made up 75 percent of all immigrants. This
trend, which had been unanticipated, has continued through
the 1980s and 1990s and has led to episodes of backlash

against immigrants, including the Vietnamese (Hein 1993: 34-37; Reimers 1992: 92-96).

One of the most highly publicized anti-Vietnamese reactions occurred along America's Gulf Coast, in Louisiana, Texas, Mississippi, and West Florida, where Vietnamese fishermen had settled. Initially a number of American seafood companies sponsored and hired Vietnamese, who, although illiterate in Vietnamese, and unable to speak English well, were skilled in fishing, making nets, and packing.

Problems arose because some Vietnamese went into business on their own, buying fishing boats and selling to companies that had not hired them. The Vietnamese were unaware of and so did not follow the laws, safety regulations, and unwritten rules and etiquette of American fishermen. They allowed their boats to bump into others, fished in areas staked out by others, used gill nets that were larger than the allowable size, and caught fish and shrimp that were undersize. Often, they worked longer and harder than the Americans, thus bringing in larger amounts for sale. All of these actions provoked the resentment of American fishermen.

As Paul Starr emphasizes, Vietnamese fishermen's violation of American laws, customs, and etiquette was unintentional, not deliberate; they were unfamiliar with American ways and unable to communicate well with Americans.

American fishermen accused the Vietnamese of competing unfairly and overusing scarce resources. False rumors circulated among the American fishermen that the U.S. government had subsidized the Vietnamese with low or interest free loans to enable them to buy boats. The coast guard instructed the Vietnamese in how to follow the law and fishing regulations, while social workers attempted to dispel the rumors and improve relations between American and Vietnamese fishermen. Most of the Vietnamese as well as the Americans responded positively, and many Americans came to praise the hard work, skill, and motivation of the Vietnamese. This did not happen everywhere. In Florida and in Louisiana, laws and local regulations were created to restrict the fishing of the Vietnamese. Some individuals, often marginally successful themselves, personally harmed or threatened the Vietnamese, shooting, sideswiping and in some cases burning their boats, cutting their nets, and refusing to sell them fuel or ice. In Seadrift, Texas, a community of 1,000 Americans and 130 refugees, two Vietnamese fishermen were acquitted of the murder of an American during a dispute. Within hours of the man's death, three Vietnamese boats were burned, one of their dwellings firebombed, and there was an attempted bombing of one of their packing houses. Two thirds of the refugees fled to another town (Starr 1981: 226-238).

Along the California coast, American and Vietnamese fishermen also clashed. In Monterey, California, where anti-Asian sentiment has simmered for decades, Vietnamese fishermen were but the latest Asian group to suffer the wrath of local fishermen.

As Vietnamese boat people began to arrive in America, reactions against them ranged from spreading rumors to intimidation and violence. Florence Baer reports that in Stockton, California, vicious rumors about the eating habits of the Vietnamese were spread by a local newspaper and an ex-mayor and member of the city council. The only Vietnamese family in an apartment complex was made a scapegoat for various problems in the complex. Angry neighbors surrounded the gate to the family's apartment and yelled at them. Soon after, the family moved away. Eventually, a voluntary agency in Stockton curtailed its resettlement program because of the "negative climate toward refugees." In hearing of the agency's announcement, the daughter of the ex-mayor remarked publicly, "If they [refugees] like swamps, we can shove them into the Delta—I know a few swamps out there" (Baer 1982: 275-291). On January 17, 1989, the Cleveland Elementary School in Stockton became the site of the worst tragedy in the history of Indochinese refugees in America. A man with an AK47 rifle murdered one Vietnamese and four Cambodian children in the schoolyard and injured 29 children and one teacher. Most of the injured children were Indochinese.

Among refugees whom I have interviewed, the majority have had cordial relations with their American neighbors, including people in Stockton and in San Jose, California where I live. But some have reported hostility directed at them. One refugee, an auto mechanic, was hit on the head with an iron bar by a black man who did not want to pay his bill. A Vietnamese unaccompanied minor walking home from school was attacked by a gang of five knife-wielding Mexican American youths shouting, "Go back to your own country, bitch!" He beat off four of them, but the fifth stabbed him in the head. I interviewed the injured youth the day after the stabbing. With his head swathed in bandages, he remarked that he was sad but harbored no ill will towards his attackers. Several elders told me of being pushed aside on the sidewalk, cursed, and threatened by hostile minority youths, who swore at them. Others told of their houses and cars being vandalized by local youths who scratched or paint-sprayed anti-Vietnamese graffiti. As I walked through a schoolyard where I was the co-director of an English instruction, job training, and job placement project for highland Laotian tribal peoples, an American asked me angrily, "Why are you helping those Vietnamese Communists?" The remark showed not only ignorance about the distinction between different Indochinese peoples, but also the misconception that the refugees were the enemy, not our allies.

CHARACTERISTICS OF THE FIRST WAVE REFUGEES

There is an extensive literature on the early resettlement of the Vietnamese refugees of 1975 (see Kelly 1977; Liu 1979; Montero 1979; Nguyen Manh Hung 1985; Stein 1979). These include surveys within the U.S. resettlement camps, eleven Reports to Congress, numerous Congressional Hearings about the refugees, and five national telephone sample surveys of the socioeconomic status, employment, education, and adjustments of Vietnamese refugees who had been resettled out of the camps by July 15, 1975. The telephone surveys were conducted under the auspices of the Department of Health, Education, and Welfare between 1975 and 1977. In the first survey, some 1570 heads of households were interviewed, drawn from a population of nearly 35,000 refugees. Later surveys used smaller samples. The surveys showed a population that tended to be young. In the first survey, over 80 percent were under the age of 35; fewer than 2 percent were over 65. It is not surprising that more males than females were found in the 18-34 age range, and that five out of every six men had been in the South Vietnamese armed forces. These military personnel would have had access to transportation out of the country.

The first survey showed that nearly three fourths of the refugees came from urban backgrounds. They tended to be fairly well educated: 48 percent of the heads of households had received high school training, and nearly 28 percent had received some university education. This made them an educational elite in Vietnam, where in 1975 less than 16 percent were in secondary school, and less than 3 percent were in the university.

The occupational backgrounds of the refugees also suggest that they were from the Vietnamese elites, or at least participants in the modern urban sector of the economy. The largest category, 24 percent, reported having professional, technical, or managerial skills; these probably included high ranking military and government officials. Next in order were transportation (17 percent), clerical and sales (12 percent), machine trades (9 percent), service (8 percent), and medical (7 percent). Only 5 percent were involved in farming or fishing, and less than 1 percent were in agricultural processing.

The refugees fled in families, often large extended families with grandparents, unmarried daughters and sons and their wives and their children. However, many families were incomplete, as relatives were separated or chose to remain in Vietnam during the period of departure. According to Immigration and Naturalization figures, around one out of eight refugees escaped alone, including several hundred unaccompanied minors.

In Vietnam, Roman Catholics numbered about 20 percent of the population. Among the refugees, however, 55 percent of those temporarily housed in Camp Pendleton, California and 40 percent at Fort Indiantown Gap said they were Catholic. (At Camp Pendleton, 27 percent listed themselves as Buddhists, 11 percent as Confucians, and 5 percent said they had no religion.) The reason for the high proportion of Catholics is that many had originally come from North Vietnam and fled South in 1954 to avoid persecution. Given their experience with the Communists in the North, Catholics feared the 1975 Communist victory in the South, and large numbers fled as refugees a second time (Kelly 1977: 41-57; Liu 1979: 43-61; Montero 1979: 21-24).

ENTERING THE WORK FORCE

At first, getting a job was a major problem for the refugees despite their previous high education and occupations (Liu 1979: 165-169). By 1977, however, according to the fifth Health, Education, and Welfare Survey, 95 percent of the men and 93 percent of the women were employed; even those without a good command of English found jobs. Of the few who were unemployed, more than a third were in school (Montero 1979: 33-55). Surveys of the entire Indochinese refugee population show significant gains in income, too. While the incomes of the 1975 first wave Indochinese refugees started out well below the national average, by 1985, their median incomes exceeded the national median income (Rumbaut 1995: 249-250).

The economic success of the Vietnamese is significant, but the American press has tended to overplay it. Failures among the Vietnamese are often underreported. The Vietnamese success story has been used to make invidious comparisons with other minorities and refugees also struggling with unemployment and poverty, with the implication that it is their own fault if they do not succeed. A more sober look at Vietnamese successes reveals that they came neither easily nor without a cost.

Many former elite Vietnamese started out as dish washers, day laborers, janitors, night watchmen, gardeners, and newspaper carriers. (Kelly 1977: 178-179; Stein 1979: 25-45). Within a few years, most had improved their incomes and upgraded their jobs, while their younger children were succeeding if not excelling in school. Colonel Tran Dinh Bui, the social worker mentioned previously, had been a highly regarded military officer whose job with the Vietnamese government had put him in contact with heads of state. In America he started out by pumping gas, then working as a garbage collector before returning to school and earning his masters degree in social work, an occupation still far lower in status than the one he had held in Vietnam. Meanwhile, his wife worked in a clothing factory. In Vietnam she had not been employed, but like many Vietnamese households in America, more than one adult needed to work to make ends meet. By choice, Colonel Bui and his family received no public assistance. Over the years, all eight of their children have earned college degrees in business or engineering, and are employed in their respective professions.

The successful first wave refugees I interviewed, like Colonel Bui, all said that their first few years in America were extremely difficult. At first, the Vietnamese were unable to get bank loans to set up new businesses because they had no credit history in America. Instead, they turned to their own community for help. Luu Trankiem's study of Vietnamese businesses in Orange county showed that 77 percent of the business owners used sources of start-up capital that came out of the refugee community. Informal circles of family and close friends accounted for most of that capital. Lending here is often based on trust, reflecting traditional ways of doing business. Only 13 percent of the initial capital came from formal financial institutions (quoted in Gold 1992: 180). Mr. Van and his wife, Mrs. Ngoc, who live in Northern California, provide one example of how first wave refugees started up businesses. In Vietnam they were a French-educated, upper middle class family, one branch of which was descended from a 19th century mandarin official. They arrived in America with no money. Mr. Van took a job in a plastics factory; after training, his wife took a job in electronics assembly; their children attended school and held part time jobs. They also did odd jobs. One time, the family painted a house, for which they received $300. Mr. Van came to know a Chinese family from Taiwan who ran a small Asian grocery shop.

Mr. Van says, "They asked me if I would like to buy the shop for $20,000. I said I had no money. They were losing money on the store, so they said they would give it to me. I took it. I was lucky to have this opportunity. I did not have a business background, but in Vietnam my wife had owned an import and export lacquer factory, and a printing shop. We built the shelves, painted new signs, and started our grocery store. We didn't know anything about permits or health regulations, but the people at the Health Department helped us and showed us what to do. We bought a 20-year old car for $200. An American friend gave me $150 and I paid $50. With the car, we would go to a nearby city, buy Asian foods with the little cash we had, and bring it back to sell in our city. Later we would drive overnight to Los Angeles, buy foods, and return home the next morning. My wife ran the store during the day and worked on the graveyard shift as an assembler. I worked the day shift in the plastics factory and ran the store during the evenings. After a few months I took a job as an educational counselor in the public schools. I also was the manager of the apartment building where we lived. Our children worked in the store after school. Then church people gave us $200, and with this, our business grew. We made a profit because all of the family members worked in the store and we did not have to pay outside wages."

Mrs. Ngoc, who was at the interview, said, "We ran the grocery store from 1976 to 1982. In 1980 we expanded and opened a little restaurant next door. I did the cooking. At the grocery store, most of our customers were Vietnamese; at the restaurant, we had both Vietnamese and American customers. After two years at the restaurant, I became tired. The grocery store was having trouble competing with new Chinese grocery stores that could undersell us. Our children were away at college and could not help us. So we closed our businesses. I went to France for six months, where I was trained as a pastry chef at a famous professional school. When I came back, I took a job as an electronics assembler. Meanwhile, my husband was attending community college for electronics technician training. Between 1985 and 1994 he worked in two large companies as a technician and a supervisor. In 1986, we opened a French bakery in an upper middle class suburb. Our customers now were mainly American. Our children helped, but we also hired a pastry chef whom we brought from France. He was expensive and insolent, so we fired him, and I took over his job. We became well known, but we did not make good profits because I used expensive ingredients. We sold the business and retired in 1991."

While the Vietnamese male elites initially experienced downward occupational, economic and social mobility, males of lower socioeconomic class, as well as females, did not suffer such a drop. Those with immediately transferable skills, such as fishermen and craftsmen, were able to find employment either in their own or related fields. Others shifted to new kinds of employment, which sometimes increased their occupational status. In places such as the Santa Clara Valley, California ("Silicon Valley"), several thousand Vietnamese were trained and took employment in electronics firms as assemblers and technicians, jobs that the Vietnamese consider middle class because they did not involve heavy physical labor (Finan 1981; 292-309).

Also in the first wave of Vietnamese refugees were a small number of older people, including some, particularly women, who did not speak any English. Their adjustments to America in every respect have been more difficult than those who are younger. Only a small percentage of older people have been employed; many are on public assistance. They do not feel at ease in the United States, and until recently they were afraid to return to visit Vietnam. Some wish to return to their homeland to die. They are heartbroken about changes in their families, including grandchildren who cannot speak Vietnamese. Both they and other elders who are more recent arrivals to the United States say they came here, not for themselves, but so that their children and grandchildren could have opportunities that were unavailable or denied to them in Vietnam.

THE BOAT PEOPLE IN AMERICA

The boat people who began to arrive in 1978 were far more diverse than the first wave Vietnamese, who were typically urban, Westernized, educated elites, many ex-military and government personnel. While the first wave refugees adjusted to America fairly quickly and easily, the adjustments of the boat people have been more varied. Many were urban ethnic Chinese. They were less highly educated and less influenced by French and American ways than many of the first wave refugees, and they had not worked in the military or the government. In Vietnam, most had held urban jobs such as shopkeepers, machine operators, factory workers, and construction workers (Whitmore 1985: 69). Other boat people who followed included many professionals such as physicians, lawyers, and teachers, as well as Buddhist and Christian monks, priests, and nuns, who, if not persecuted, were often singled out for discrimination in Communist Vietnam. Former reeducation camp prisoners, who had escaped or been released from the camps, also fled. In addition, the boat people included students, farmers, fishermen, craftsmen and laborers, youths fleeing the military draft for the Cambodia conflict, business people, and children sent out by their parents in the hopes that they would have a better future. They had lower levels of education, fewer material resources and job skills, less knowledge of English, and less contact with American ways than the first wave refugees.

The Indochina Migration and Refugee Assistance Act of 1975, provided one-time funding to assist in the resettlement of Vietnamese and other refugees from Indochina. In 1977, the Act was reauthorized to continue temporary funding for refugees. The funds came, not from welfare, but from the special legislation just mentioned, which was voted on by Congress. The special social welfare status of the refugees tended to be blurred with that of ordinary welfare because refugee assistance came through the Department of Health and Human Services. There were other differences from welfare. Although refugees had to meet income or resource eligibility criteria of Aid to Families with Dependent Children (which provides assistance to single parent families or families in which the second parent is unemployable), refugee mothers with husbands as well as couples without children were entitled to receive aid for families. This special consideration was carried over into the 1980 Refugee Act in the form of Refugee Cash Assistance for three years, subsequently reduced to 18 months in 1982, and, since 1992, to 8 months. This is a federal program administered through each state. Some states or local areas also have General Assistance programs for poor

residents, including refugees. In 1980, the Refugee Act established the Office of Refugee Resettlement (ORR) in the Department of Health and Human Services. The ORR funds
private and public organizations to provide social services to
refugees and has financed a number of studies to examine
how successful their programs have been in helping refugees
become economically self sufficient.

Because most refugees arrived without any money, public assistance helped them to survive during their initial adjustments in the United States. Of particular importance were
programs of English language instruction and job training
which were intended to develop economic self-sufficiency for
refugees. A high percentage of newly arrived Vietnamese,
but an even higher percentage of other Indochinese refugees
(Cambodians, Laotian lowlanders, Laotian tribal highland-
ers), began on public assistance. By 1982, 80 percent of all Indochinese refugees who had been in the United States for one
and a half years were receiving cash assistance. Such assistance continued to be important for families during their first
five years of residence in America. In 1990, 25.7 percent of all
Vietnamese families had an income below the poverty level;
24.5 percent were receiving some public assistance (for California, see Department of Social Services 1993). The poverty
rate for Vietnamese was twice the national average (Rumbaut
1995: 247-248; Le Ngoan 1994: 12). For the most part, the Vietnamese poor were the new arrivals. Significantly, the use of
public assistance declined over time, especially as the refugees learned English (Hein 1993: 56-58). The few who continue to receive long-term assistance tend to be the elderly and
those with health problems.

As a rule, household income grows and poverty rates de-
cline as the length of residence in the United States increases
(Le Ngoan 1994: 13). In a study of Vietnamese, ethnic Chinese, and Laotian refugees, Caplan and his colleagues found
that 80 percent of the families were below the poverty level in
their first year in the United States, but only 31 percent remained there after three and a half years. Steady economic
improvement came when households combined the earned
incomes of two or more workers with the cash assistance
given newly arrived relatives who had joined the household.

As individuals took employment, their cash assistance was reduced and finally terminated when their earned incomes exceeded a certain level (Caplan et al. 1989: 51-64; Caplan et al. 1991: 58-70; see also Rumbaut 1995: 249-252).

Voluntary agencies have played a major role in the resettlement of refugees and helping them get jobs. These agencies have contracts funded by the federal government to provide services such as English instruction, job training, job placement, cultural adjustment, and social and mental health counseling. Unfortunately, as Gold notes, these agencies are often "inefficient in terms of coordination and allocation of funding, and sometimes created interagency competition and hostility" (Gold 1992: 145, 159). Networks created by the refugees themselves often provide greater help in getting jobs and in providing emotional support than the voluntary agencies (Gold 1992: 149).

Santa Clara County, California, provides an example of the problems faced by new arrivals, even with a wide array of programs available. English instruction and job training programs frequently did not take into account refugee needs, values, and habits. For some groups, drop out rates were high; job placement was low, and no follow-ups were made to see how long the refugees kept their jobs. An exception was a program specifically designed to meet the needs of refugees from Highland Laos. What distinguished this program was its participatory character: adult refugee students were involved in decision making, hiring of personnel, and, when they were ready, in taking over responsibility for job placement for their own people (Freeman, Nguyen, and Hartsell 1985). Despite ample money being poured into several agencies, many Vietnamese refugees and immigrants in Santa Clara County were unable to find and secure basic medical, legal, and counseling services. Although a directory had been compiled for them, they had no idea how to use it; they were unable to find agencies they needed to reach or call for emergency services. Mr. Tran Dinh Bui, the social worker, on his own time put together a directory and cultural orientation, with step-by-step instructions on how to use the directory.

Nazli Kibria notes that recent arrivals from Vietnam, especially women, tend to take jobs that are part-time, unstable, without fringe benefits, and without opportunities for advancement. Women frequently work in the areas of manufacturing garments or preparing food. Many Vietnamese refugees and immigrants prefer to work in the informal or underground economy, even though the pay often is below minimum wage and health and safety conditions are below minimum standards. But the hours are flexible, they do not pay taxes, they do not come under the scrutiny of welfare and social services agencies, and they often can work at home (Kibria 1993:77-107).

Because refugees are given government assistance for only a short time, they are soon pushed out into the workplace seeking low level jobs with little chance of advancement. In her study of Vietnamese and Laotians working in the meat packing industry in Garden City, Kansas, Janet Benson observes that the companies seek to hire Southeast Asian women as a source of cheap labor. Southeast Asian women are believed to be more docile than men and other ethnic groups. As refugees, Southeast Asians have nowhere to return to, have minimal educational skills, and a low educational level.

For these reasons, they do not have the possibilities of alternative employment as do some other groups. It also makes them vulnerable to abuse. If they become ill or injured, or if they take time off for an emergency, they are often immediately fired. Worker's Compensation is made so complicated and formidable that most injured workers move away looking for employment elsewhere rather than pursue their case. They put up with substandard housing in order to be able to work at the plant, and they take in boarders to help defray costs. One adult earning low wages cannot earn enough to support a family with several dependents, so husbands and wives both work. If they take unusual hours, they receive overtime pay. They earn in order to survive, send money back to relatives in their homeland, sponsor relatives to come to America, and to accumulate capital to invest in education for their children, purchase their own businesses, or buy material possessions (Benson 1994: 99-126).

Because of the obstacles they had to overcome and the cultural distances they had to bridge, the achievements of the boat people are even more impressive than those of the first wave refugees. An example is Mr. Liem, who was a farmer and fisherman, born in a central Vietnamese Catholic village. He came to the United States in late 1978 with no job skills, hardly any education, and without any knowledge of English. For five months, his family remained with his brother, who had sponsored them; then they moved to a town in another part of the country, where for nine months he and his wife studied English. They received public assistance, but it was insufficient to live on, even though they bought ragged second-hand clothes. In 1980, Mr. Liem moved to a farming town in California where one of his sisters was living. Mr. Liem worked as a farm laborer and grew vegetables in the back yard of the house he rented. He and his wife used some of the vegetables and sold the rest to their neighbors; then they expanded to a farmer's market. Two years later, he bought a truck and started a business in which he sells fish. At first, he had no idea that he needed permits, but Americans helped him; now he fills out all the paperwork himself. As his income grew, his public assistance was reduced; when I interviewed him in 1983, his family was receiving less than $15 a month. He and his wife were looking forward to being off of public assistance entirely. When asked to account for his success, Mr. Liem remarked, "God made me a hard-working man.". Although he lived in a town notorious for ethnic tensions and anti-immigrant sentiment, he and his ethnically diverse neighbors were close friends who trusted one another (Freeman 1989: 382-390).

By 1993, Mr. Liem's sister and her family, who also started out growing vegetables, owned two large grocery stores and their own house. His brother who had sponsored him also owned his own house and a big boat, which his family used for fishing. Mr. Liem's brother had given him one piece of advice to succeed in America, "You should not receive public assistance; you should go to work."

Hard work and efforts at self-improvement characterize many of the boat people and the earlier first wave arrivals. Miss That Thao, a forties-something single Vietnamese woman, exemplifies this. Her father died in a reeducation camp after three years of suffering. She tried ten times to escape from Vietnam before she succeeded. It cost her $2000. Her boat was stopped and pillaged three times by pirates before reaching Thailand. In 1981, a Catholic priest sponsored her resettlement in the United States. She lives in California. She remained on public assistance only for two months. She did not have enough money to send anything back to Vietnam to help her brothers and sisters, so she dropped public assistance and took a job as a photo technician, which she still holds. In 1983 she bought her first home. In 1988, Miss Thao bought her second home, a spiffy condo in a neighborhood of rising middle class professionals.

Despite being separated from her family, Miss Thao finds America to be "like heaven." Because she is alone, she has ups and downs. She becomes desperately lonely during the Vietnamese New Year, a time of family reunion. To fill her time, she holds two full time jobs. During the day, she is a counselor for Vietnamese students at a vocational college. She also takes classes there. During the swing shift, she works at the photo lab. For several years she also sang with a band, and she still does occasional concerts. Her schedule is hectic: vocational counseling from 10 A.M. to 5 P.M.; the photo technician job from 10 P.M. to 6 A.M. from Sunday through Thursday; then three hours of sleep from 6:30-9:30 A.M. She studies mutual fund investing on Wednesday night and Saturday morning, and she earns commissions. On Wednesday night she gets no sleep. Her only free nights are Friday and Saturday. She enrolls in motivational seminars on self-improvement. "In Vietnam, we waste a lot of time. We gossip a lot and drink coffee for two or three hours. I want to spend my time differently, smarter. In America I learn to manage my time and use it well. I used to be shy and insecure. Now I am very open and confident in myself. I believe I get better every day. Nothing can stop me; I can do what I want."

ODP IMMIGRANTS, HO ARRIVALS, AND POST-CPA REFUGEES

You may recall that the Orderly Departure Program (ODP) was established in the early 1980s to encourage legal emigration rather than illegal escape from Vietnam. Since that time, many people have come to the United States as ODP immigrants. Like the first wave and boat people refugees, the earlier ODP immigrants over time have improved their standard of living. By contrast, the more recent ODP, HO, and post-CPA arrivals tend to live well below the poverty line. They have few marketable skills, have little or no knowledge of English, and find it hard to get jobs or adequate vocational training. If they come from rural areas, their children had minimal education in Vietnam and initially have had a hard time adjusting in American schools. Many suffered grievously in Vietnam. They come with high, often unrealistic expectations that America is the land of easy and unlimited opportunity. They expect to make money right away and to have an easy life. They find instead that they live in grinding poverty in a bewildering new land. They frequently become discouraged. When they complain to their Vietnamese relatives who have been here longer, have worked hard for years to get where they are, and have sacrificed to sponsor the new arrivals, they often do not receive a sympathetic ear.

Such is the case with Mr. An Thu, a 60 year old, well educated central Vietnamese male from a traditional high status family whom I interviewed in June, 1994, six months after he and his family had come to the United States as ODP immigrants. We talked in the dingy living room of the house he rented from his wife's cousin. The small house was in a dusty, run-down neighborhood of a large West Coast city. The front yard was overrun with tall, dry grass. The paint on the outside walls of the house was peeling, and the windows were smudged. Inside, the walls were stained, the sofa was torn and lumpy, and the wooden chairs were broken. Soiled clothes were strewn all over the house.

Mr. An Thu himself looked frail and forlorn, beaten down, and when he spoke, his words were bitter. He had been one of the thousands of South Vietnamese army officers left behind when the Communists won the war. He recalls how he felt when they arrived, "I had no feelings at all; I accepted what would come to me. This was the destiny of our country. I expected to be imprisoned. After clearing trees and constructing the reeducation camp to which I had been sent, I was forced to clear the fields and remove the mines, which occasionally exploded and killed us prisoners. Then I planted corn and vegetables, very hard work for me because I was in my forties and living on starvation rations. I was depressed, but I didn't want to commit suicide. Thinking of my family, I did not dare. And when I ran across a mine and picked it up, I thought, 'whatever happens will happen. If it explodes, then I die, but I won't kill myself.'" He was released after two and a half years.

Meanwhile, his family had been sent to a New Economic Zone, where they did hard labor, and he rejoined them. He was not allowed back in Saigon. In 1982, his family tried to flee Vietnam but they were caught and imprisoned. Along with 260 men, he was in a room 20 by 60 feet. "There was no room to move; we slept sitting up. Food consisted of one-half of a coconut shell of rice twice a day." After one year, he was released because there were too many prisoners to house.

His family remained in a New Economic Zone until 1986. Then in his fifties, he no longer had the energy to work in the fields. Also, his children had received no education. So without asking permission from the authorities, his family moved back to Saigon, where they lived by doing whatever jobs they could find. "I repaired bicycles, worked as a bicycle rickshaw driver, bought and sold cans and bottles, sold bread, lots of things. And my wife did whatever she could. We had very little food, no medicine, and our clothes were old and tattered left-overs from pre-Communist days."

In 1987, the United States and Vietnam agreed to resettle all former reeducation camp prisoners and their families, provided that the prisoners had been incarcerated for at least three years. They would be brought to the United States under the Humanitarian Operation Program. Mr. An Thu applied, but was rejected because he had not been in the camps for at least three years. In 1992, his sister-in-law in the United States sponsored his family, and in December 1993, they arrived in America.

Mr. An Thu was considered an ODP immigrant, not an HO reeducation camp arrival. "I'm not allowed to receive money for a while, but I don't know for how long. My children also were not given money to go to school. I am disappointed. I had hoped to receive assistance just like others who were in reeducation camps. When I arrived, I felt the government discriminated against me because I came out of the camp before three years. Before I came here, I thought my sons could go to the university; they are anxiously awaiting the chance. But they don't have the money. In Vietnam, one had been studying economics, while another had completed a year of engineering. In Vietnam, even if they had graduated, they would not have been allowed to hold a job because I was a former officer in the South Vietnamese army. Here in America, the eldest is a solderer, the second has been laid off, and the third works in an electronics company. My wife works part-time, while I stay home, driving them to work and cooking for them and for the people from whom we rent. I have friends from military days. I talk to them on the phone. I don't have my own house yet, so I don't feel comfortable having them over."

He is unhappy that his relatives who sponsored him had not done more for him. He concludes sadly, "We feel like we are at the bottom of society, especially those of us who are older. In Vietnam, everyone respects the elderly, but not in America. I don't have anything here. But with the Viet Cong [the term South Vietnamese people use to refer to the Communists], I had to come here. Vietnamese people have one important custom. Parents sacrifice for their children. And that's what I have done; I have sacrificed for them. As for me, I don't have any more feelings about myself. I only hope that my children can slowly get education here. My generation has already passed. Now I do what I can to help my children go forward. They really enjoy being here because they have a future."

The sons, however, were not so optimistic about their prospects. The first son, 24 years old, who had completed one year of law school and two years of business administration in Vietnam, said, "Before I left Vietnam, I thought it would be easy to work and make more money in the United States. But when I came here, I found it was very difficult because of my language difficulties. I cannot speak English, so I cannot do anything." For a few months, he had been a solderer and welder, but he slipped, broke a bone, and was not working. He said, "To live in America is to be boxed in. In Vietnam, I used to be outside a lot, but here I'm indoors and I feel unhealthy and restless. In Vietnam we lacked material things but felt at ease; in America, we have material things, but emotionally we don't feel at ease. Here we have responsibility, we must go to work on time; when I return home, I eat and worry about going back to sleep for the next day. Life is just like a circle here. We just go round and round."

The second son, 22 years old, who had been laid off from his low-wage electronics assembly job, expressed even deeper disappointment about living in America, "Life is very difficult because I cannot speak English. I don't have a car, so it's very hard to get around. We have no home in which to feel comfortable. Where we live is just a temporary dwelling. In America, you have to work hard to have money. Americans just work and work, without playing; they don't have feelings, they are cold. In Vietnam, I used to eat a lot, but here in America, I don't feel like it. I hate American food. My appetite just is not there, I have poor energy, fatigue, and I am losing weight."

The third son, 19, an electronics assembler, was more upbeat, though disappointed in his Vietnamese relatives. "I want to speak English to get a good job, but I am unable. I miss Vietnam, but I like working here and I like it better here. The big trouble for all of us is English. Vietnamese people who have been here a while don't have the patience to show us new arrivals around, to explain how life is. And our relatives are all over the place, not near, so we cannot ask them for help."

Their mother, who is 15 years younger than their father, likes the United States. Within days of her arrival, she cut and permed her hair, bought more stylish clothes, and got a job assembling electronic games. She is adjusting rapidly to the United States, especially to the new individualism and economic self-sufficiency that her new job brings.

DIVERSITY OF VIETNAMESE OCCUPATIONS AND THE NEW PROFESSIONALS

After 20 years in America, the Vietnamese hold a wide variety of occupations based on their education, length of time in the United States, and location in the United States. In many communities, the Vietnamese are in relatively low level and low paying occupations. In a study of the Vietnamese of eastern New Orleans, Min Zhou and Carl Bankston observed that the highest percentage of Vietnamese were employed as cashiers, waiters and waitresses, cooks, fishers, and textile sewing machine operators, and that such blue collar occupations are typical of Vietnamese communities throughout America (Zhou and Bankston 1994: 830). In Santa Clara County, California, although the majority of Vietnamese workers are in blue collar occupations, the distribution of occupations is somewhat different. In 1990, out of more than 20,000 Vietnamese people who were employed (19 percent of the Vietnamese workforce of California), 38 percent were in technician, sales and clerical positions, 23 percent in the engineering and health professions, 18 percent in machine operation and assembly, 10 percent in mechanics and precision production jobs, 11 percent in services, including food, and one percent in farming and fishing. Because Santa Clara County is in the heart of "Silicon Valley," large numbers of Vietnamese in the first three categories were employed in high tech companies, in blue collar and managerial positions, and increasing numbers of health professionals were setting up practices. There were 1645 Vietnamese engineers, 478 computer scientists, 289 managers, 2272 secretaries and administrative support people, 2472 engineering and science technicians, 1299 other technicians, and 1422 assemblers.

One Vietnamese said to me, "The Vietnamese are the backbone of the high tech industry in Silicon Valley. In some companies, if you want to be promoted to manager, you need to be able to speak Vietnamese. If the Vietnamese workers left, the companies would collapse." In addition, there were 58 Vietnamese physicians, 45 other health-diagnosing profes-

sionals, 62 other health assessment and treating professionals, and 21 attorneys (1990 Census, California, Santa Clara
County: PB16-PB18). The Vietnamese say that in the five
years since the 1990 Census, the numbers of Vietnamese physicians, dentists, and engineers in Silicon Valley have increased sharply.

In striking contrast to the quickly disillusioned new immigrants, young Vietnamese professionals trained in the
United States are likely to be optimistic and confident about
the future. Unlike their parents, they are not overwhelmed by
the sorrows of the past or the changes taking place in the Vietnamese American community. Many of them also are active
community service volunteers, another contrast to their parents.

Alexander Hao Nguyen, D.D.S. exemplifies this new outlook. He changed his name to Alexander and refers to himself
as Alex, "so that Americans would not have to ask me how to
spell my name." Dr. Nguyen was born in Saigon in 1968, the
youngest in the family; he has six sisters and two brothers. In
1979, his father died, and soon after, he and his family escaped to Thailand; from there, they were resettled in California. His family expected him to do well in school. Because he
was studious, no one in the family watched over his studies.
While he liked science, his first love was music, especially
playing the piano; he knew, however, that his mother looked
down on performers as slightly disreputable and unlikely to
earn a steady income. "By the eighth grade, I knew that I
wanted to become a dentist, combining both science and art."
With stress and effort, he completed dental school at the age
of 25 and opened a practice which caters mainly to Vietnamese patients. He is the first in his family to have become a
modern health professional. His mother and siblings are
proud of his achievements, and he knows that some Vietnamese envy his prestigious profession with a comfortable income. "What they don't realize," he says, "are the stresses
which go along with my profession. They think my job is easy
and without worries, but it is not."

Dr. Nguyen contrasts his outlook with the more conservative generation of his parents. "They look to the past. I look to
the future. They expect us to marry within the Vietnamese

community. For me, being Vietnamese is not a requirement for marriage. When I have children, I would not expect them to marry a Vietnamese. In my generation, we have lost some of the old ways. We are able to mix more freely with other Americans. Still, if you ask me how I identify myself, I'll tell you I'm Vietnamese, not American, even though I have lived here since the age of 12. At the office, I'm an American, but at home and deep inside me I remain Vietnamese."

Dr. Nguyen believes that core values of the Vietnamese will be retained by the next generation in America, especially respect for parents, studiousness, hard work, and maintaining family ties. Because of this, he is optimistic about the continuing economic successes of Vietnamese Americans. He advertises on Vietnamese radio shows with public service announcements concerning dental care. He and some college friends are doing a radio show to explain to parents and students the importance of attending college and the process for applying.

Dr. Nguyen attributes his success and positive outlook to hard work and high self-esteem. "Without self-esteem, it is easy to become discouraged. I have several friends who quit trying; their self esteem was low, and their families created stresses that interfered with their studying. As a teenager, I had low self esteem. I wanted to be like all the other kids, to hide my Vietnamese identity. Now I realize that I am Vietnamese, and that the Vietnamese have a lot to offer America."

5

Education: Aiming for Success

ACADEMIC ACHIEVEMENTS

The academic achievements of Vietnamese schoolchildren in America are almost legendary: valedictorians of high schools and colleges, a Rhodes scholar, winners of science competitions, high grade point averages, high scores on the Scholastic Aptitude (now Assessment) Test. This is especially impressive given that many Vietnamese students came to America as boat people who survived perilous escapes and lost one to three years in refugee camps, where they had little schooling. A majority come from families in which adults speak limited or no English. A quarter of the families live below the poverty level and attend poor schools in low-income areas. Yet within three to five years in the United States, many students have excelled, performing scholastically at a level higher than many U.S. and foreign-born students.

The accomplishments are real; they represent the achievements, not of a select few who stand out, but of many Vietnamese students throughout the country. At the same time, not all Vietnamese students are doing well; some are dropping out, while others have no more than average records.

In 1981 and 1984, Caplan, Whitmore, and Choy followed the progress of Vietnamese, ethnic Chinese, and Laotian stu-

dents in Boston, Houston, Seattle, Chicago, and Orange
County, California. As reported in the previous chapter, the
households they studied were showing steady economic
progress over several years. The schoolchildren in these
households also achieved impressive results. In overall grade
point average, 27 percent were A students, 52 percent B, 17
percent C, and only 4 percent D or below. The overall grade
point average was 3.05, a B average. In math, 47 percent were
in the A range, 32 percent B, 15 percent C and 6 percent D or
below. Science grades were also high, with 56 percent in the
B or A range. Lower scores were seen in those courses which
required greater use of English. Students in higher grades did
just about as well as those in the lower grades. On standardized achievement tests, such as the California Achievement
Test (CAT), the refugee children performed as well or better
than the national average, though they tended to be over-rep-
resented in the middle ranges. What pulled them down were
the language and reading scores; the refugee children had
been in the United States on average about three and a half
years and they came from homes in which no one had been
able to speak English when they arrived in the United States.
In math, however, where English was not as important, the
students did extremely well: 27 percent of the refugee students were in the top 10 percent nationally and half were in
the top 25 percent; only 15 percent were in the bottom fifty
percent of students nationally (Caplan, Whitmore, and Choy
1989: 65-75; Caplan, Choy, and Whitmore 1991: 5-14).

In San Diego, California, Ruben Rumbaut has conducted
a number of studies of the educational attainment of Indochinese youth. He found that among all the groups in the school
district he studied, "the Indochinese have by far the largest
proportion of LEP [Limited English Proficiency] students, reflecting the fact that they are the most recently arrived immigrants. Despite the language handicap, however, their
academic grade point averages (GPAs) (2.47) significantly exceed the district average (2.11) and that of white Anglos
(2.24)." Among the Indochinese students, the Vietnamese
scored highest, with those fluent in English achieving at a significantly higher level than those whose English was limited.
In GPA, the Vietnamese outperformed all groups except Chi-

nese, Korean, East Indian, and what Rumbaut terms Hebrew students (Rumbaut 1995: 262, based on Portes and Rumbaut 1990: 189-198). In standardized achievement tests, the Vietnamese scored higher in math and lower in reading than the district average (Portes and Rumbaut 1990: 196-197). When Rumbaut and Ima looked at Indochinese refugee students in San Diego who had been in the United States a period of three to six years, they found that the younger the students and the longer they had been in United States schools, the higher their GPA. Students fluent in English were more successful than the less fluent. The mother's psychological stresses affected the students: the higher her stresses, the lower the GPAs of the students. Families which did not buy wholeheartedly into American ways produced students whose grade point averages were higher than those who Americanized more completely, in other words, "Americanization may be counterproductive for educational attainment" (Rumbaut 1995: 265; Rumbaut and Ima 1988).

VALUES FOR SUCCESS

How did these refugee students, who had been in America such a short time, achieve academic results equal to or better than American children? According to Caplan and his colleagues, ethnicity, religion, gender, and socioeconomic status and past education of parents do not explain the "startling and extraordinary" progress by these refugee children who have been in the United States only a short time (Caplan, Choy, and Whitmore 1991: 15-17). The answer lies in the values the refugee families brought with them. When the researchers asked the refugee families what values they held to be the most important, 98 percent cited education and achievement, a cohesive family, and hard work. The researchers call these core values. Ninety percent of the families listed a cluster of other values: Family loyalty, freedom, morality and ethics, carrying out obligations, restraint and discipline, emphasis on perpetuating the ancestral lineage, respect for elders, and a cooperative and harmonious family. The two values that they rated as least important were fun and excitement and material possessions; ninety-five percent of the respondents listed those two values at the bottom. In contrast, they thought that those two values were the ones most highly rated by their nonrefugee neighbors (Caplan, Choy, and Whitmore 1991: 76-79). In fact, the study revealed a fundamental difference in value orientation between the American middle class and Vietnamese refugees: Americans stress individualistic achievement and competitiveness whereas the refugees emphasize cooperation and collective achievement, seen first in the family, and then applied to the school environment (Caplan, Choy, and Whitmore 1991: 131-132). However, it should be noted that in many endeavors the Vietnamese are quite competitive individually and are not invariably cooperative.

At the center of refugee children's success is the family, an institution of great importance to them. Caplan, Choy, and Whitmore show that high achievement occurs in those refugees families, first, in which spouses develop relative equality in participation in the labor force, decision making, and in involvement in school-related activities; second, where there is parental involvement in the child's education, such as reading to the child and supervising homework; third, where parents exert discipline and control over their children which is firm but not harsh. In families with high-achieving children, parents urged children to do well for the pride of the family; gave the children self-confidence by telling them they had the ability to do well; rewarded good performance with presents or privileges; and stressed shame if the children fell below expectations (Caplan, Choy, and Whitmore 1991: 98-107).

The authors conclude with a critical look at mainstream or middle class values in the United States. "It has often been assumed," they say, "that successful adaptation by refugees was, in large measure, the result of their willingness to adopt the ways of their American neighbors. But the successes of these refugees...may have occurred for opposite reasons." Indochinese parents cited two major obstacles that held back their children in school: first English comprehension, and second, disruption by nonrefugee children. "The implication is to reject rather than emulate the ways of their nonrefugee neighbors. Perhaps the refugees see not only the necessity to rely on their own cultural value system for guidance but also the need to insulate themselves from the behavioral and value standards of their nonrefugee neighbors" (Caplan, Choy, and Whitmore 1991: 131).

Zhou and Bankston arrive at similar conclusions in their study of second generation Vietnamese youth living in a poor, biracial New Orleans neighborhood. The most successful youth are those who are influenced by family and community not to become too "American." They show "strong adherence to traditional family values, a strong commitment to a work ethic, a high level of ethnic involvement, and a weak adherence to egoistic family values," defined as "to think for oneself and be popular." The success of an individual is a family and community endeavor. A parent said to the authors, "my children know that if they become doctor or become engineer, I share it with them, and our friends and neighbors share it. But if they fail, we all fail" (Zhou and Blankston 1994: 821-845).

Vietnamese refugees also tell me that they try to insulate themselves from lower class minorities, whom they associate with low education and poor paying jobs. Young Vietnamese women are encouraged to marry educated men who are *su* and *si*—a reference to endings in the Vietnamese language for titles such as physician, dentist, lawyer, engineer, and professor.

CONTINUITIES AND CHANGES IN VIETNAMESE EDUCATION AND VALUES

What are the origins of Vietnamese attitudes to education? Many Vietnamese families who came to America did not expect their children to be able to pursue education, especially higher education, in their home country. Education, especially the higher levels, historically was for the elites, not the masses, though at certain times gifted lower class students were allowed to compete. An education was highly valued, and an educated man was held in the highest esteem. Since the eleventh century A.D., education had been associated with Chinese-style civil service examinations, at first based both on Chinese classical writings and Buddhist texts, but by the 15th century mainly on Chinese Confucian texts. These exams continued until the 20th century. In villages, teachers, often themselves previously failed candidates, prepared the students for the exams, and a student learned to respect and obey his teacher without question. "Emperor, Teacher, Father," states one proverb, indicating the order in which respect should be given. Another proverb states, "First learn moral behavior, then learn literature." Education begins with proper moral behavior without which a person is not educated.

Alexander Woodside has described these exams as they were conducted in the 19th century. Lower-level exams were held every year. Ideally, though not always in fact, the highest level exam, the Palace exam, was held every three years. For the lower exams, village chiefs had to certify to district officials that the candidates were morally suitable; those who were "unfilial, inharmonious, or rebellious were not to be included"(Woodside 1988: 177). The candidate should possess or begin to approximate the qualities of the ideal Confucian man, such as benevolence, righteousness, and proper etiquette.

The exams were dramatic and spectacular events which lasted nearly two weeks. They symbolized the unification of the country in that the successful graduates, drawn from different regions, became the mandarins, the high ranking officials who ran the country. The examination sites were usually large rectangular fields surrounded by bamboo fences, and divided into two sections, one for the examiners, and one where the candidates pitched their tents and took their exams. A watchtower stood between the two sections. A more permanent exam site with brick structures was built in the capital city of Hue. A complex bureaucracy managed the event, involving eight or nine levels of examiners, along with "two censors and a corps of military investigators and inspectors. Copyists, sealers, proofreaders, ordinary bureaucrats and soldiers were also present....There might be 48 different ranking officials at large sites like Hanoi and Hue"(Woodside 1988: 198). The announcement of the successful graduates usually took place ten days after the completion of the exams.

The national triennial exam, which drew candidates from all over the country, was a sort of intellectual Super Bowl or World Cup Soccer event, with the winners of the doctorate its superstars. Graduates at different levels earned titles that had enormous prestige, which carried over to their families, as well as to the villages from which they came. Villagers were proud of having produced successful graduates. The wife of a successful graduate shared his title, and, as Woodside has observed, "she participated in the triumphal procession, which his village neighbors were required to tender him after he had won his degree, from the provincial capital back to his native village....The procession itself was called a 'glorious return.' Expensive to the villagers as a social burden they could not avoid, it gave rise to the cynical saying, 'The student who has not yet passed his doctoral examinations is already a threat to his canton neighbors'" (Woodside 1988: 171).

In Hanoi, carved stone slabs inscribed with the names of successful graduates at the doctoral level stand inside the Temple of Literature, dedicated to Confucius and built in the 11th century AD. They represent the pinnacle of achievement in education. A favorite story among many Vietnamese is that of Pham Cong, who starts out as an orphan and buffalo boy at the lowest rung of society, but, through his extraordinary talents achieves not only status as a great warrior, but even an even higher status as scholar-gentleman, winner of the doctorate and therefore appointed a mandarin. This achievement might have been out of reach for most people, but the ideal lived on in ritual, legend, and the saying, "Every boy dreams of becoming a mandarin."

Confucian-style education is long gone, and so are many of its values. But traces have remained despite momentous changes over the past century. The last Chinese-style civil servant exam in Vietnam took place in 1918. By that time, French-style education was replacing the old system and introducing new Western values, the French language, and a French curriculum, along with scientific and humanistic subjects. Still, under colonialism, education was only for the favored few. The great majority of Vietnamese were illiterate. Only two public high schools existed in all of Vietnam, though there were exclusive private schools of various kinds for the elites. A refugee, born in 1906, who attended a teacher's college in the 1920s, claims that the French made education as difficult as possible for the Vietnamese. "The French were afraid the Vietnamese students would get too much education and then would resist them, so they tried to hold us back. The books used by French kids were much easier than our texts, and their exam results were lower than ours. But they got a 'French' diploma and we got a 'Vietnamese' diploma. In spite of the French attempts to hold us back, we were not less intelligent, and we did better because we made a greater effort." (Freeman 1989: 42-43).

Not until the French left Vietnam in 1954 did education begin to open up to a wider spectrum of students, and the Vietnamese language was now used in the schools along with French. In South Vietnam, there was a great increase in those who attended high school and college, though the numbers were still relatively small. More females now were teachers. Still, strict discipline remained; students were expected to show their teachers respect, to pay attention, and behave properly. A refugee recalls the school environment of the early 1970s: "Our teacher was about 50 years old and very strict. We treated her with great respect. After entering the classroom, we'd stand until the teacher arrived and gave us permission to sit down. As a mark of respect, we crossed our arms on our chests, and when she spoke to us, we responded by saying, 'Respected Teacher'" (Freeman 1989: 103).

Under Communist rule in North Vietnam, where education was used as a means of political persuasion, the emphasis was on extending basic literacy and providing a Marxist education. After 1975, with the Communist victory throughout Vietnam, many students whose families were politically suspect were denied education, especially at higher levels. Impoverished rural areas had virtually no books or materials, teachers were so underpaid that they usually held several jobs to make ends meet, and school buildings often went unrepaired. In 1986, the Renovation policy, which liberalized the economy, also led to a revamping of education, with greater emphasis on contemporary subjects. The English language is now taught beginning in the first grade, though the emphasis is on grammar and reading rather than on oral communication. There has been a steady increase in the number and percent of six to ten-year olds who attend primary school, up to 87 percent in 1991-1992. However, only 60 percent completed the first five years. Students from politically incorrect families no longer are denied higher education, though many still claim that they are denied jobs after they complete their schooling. The main problems in improving education continue to be lack of funds, a serious shortage of qualified teachers and materials, and the low salaries of teachers. Teachers end up moonlighting, and parents have to pay for books, materials, and the maintenance of school buildings (Socialist Republic of Vietnam 1992: 48-51). Students coming to America from areas where there is deficient schooling have difficulty in adjusting.

Through all the changes in Vietnamese society in the past century, certain behaviors and values concerning education have persisted, and the Vietnamese have brought them to the United States. There is a great love and enthusiasm for learning, as well as enormous respect for and a tradition of absolute obedience to teachers. Students are taught not to question but to receive and accept the knowledge and information that teachers impart. Also deeply ingrained are enormous respect and admiration for persons who are educated. Families have a deep, unquestioned commitment to support the pursuit of an education. And there is a long tradition of admiring and longing for higher education, something from which most people were excluded. What has changed in America is that Vietnamese now have the opportunity to get a higher education. Considering what so many refugees and immigrants have gone through to get here, the opportunities available in America, both economic and educational, are more than they could ever have imagined, and they are taking advantage of them.

PROFILES OF SUCCESS AND FAILURE

How do the values I have just described come into play in the day-to-day lives of Vietnamese refugees and immigrants? The children of first wave refugee parents include successes as well as failures in school. In the first two examples below, I compare a successful female engineer with a male businessman who at first struggled in school but later pulled himself together. In both cases, family environment and values influenced them. An older sibling is expected to be a role model for younger brothers and sisters. A widely held belief is that the behavior of the older sibling sets the direction that other siblings will follow. This places great pressure on older children to meet the expectations of their parents; failure to do so leads to family conflicts. Major sources of tension are failure to succeed in school, refusal to follow the career direction parents choose for the child, and selection of spouses who do not meet parental approval. In the third example, I describe a recently arrived unaccompanied minor who is bounced from one foster home to another. Although quite bright, she is failing in school. She receives no parental guidance but lives virtually on her own. Her friends contribute to her problems in school, and school authorities are indifferent or hostile to her plight.

In 1994, I first met Quynh Thi Nga, 29, who had become an electrical engineer, hardly a traditional career path for Vietnamese women. Nga is the third of seven children, four sisters and three brothers, but the only one who has become an engineer. Their educational and occupational histories reflect their different ages and the greater opportunity for the younger siblings to become competent in English and obtain higher education. The two oldest, a sister and a brother in their early thirties, each completed two years of community college and work as electronic technicians, a job requiring some technical training but not much English. The next three children (a group which includes Nga), each have completed college degrees: a sister is a school teacher, and a brother, with an accounting degree, is a security officer. The two youngest siblings are attending university. The youngest, 21, with interests in public relations and art history, "is the most Americanized. She has many American friends and follows American ways. She follows tradition in that she studies hard, but unlike the rest of us, she studies what she likes. It's only natural; she was only one and a half when she came to America. She understands the Vietnamese language but can only speak it a little bit."

Nga was born in Vietnam and lived there until 1975, when at the age of ten she and her middle class urban family escaped to the United States. She recalls going to a public school in Vietnam attended by both boys and girls. She does not remember any values being taught in school other than being polite to elders. Her dominant memory is that the teacher punished children by hitting them with a ruler. At home, she learned that "Teacher was second to Father, and Father was second to God. [She reverses the usual order of precedence: Emperor, Teacher, Father]. I obeyed Father, but I was also taught self-sufficiency, not to be spoiled, but to take care of myself. My brothers and sisters were brought up about the same; we would be beaten with rattan if we misbehaved. My brothers got into trouble more often. When we were punished, we had to stand, cross our arms, and then we were beaten."

When Nga's family came to America, they lived for two years in a couple of small towns on the West Coast in which there were only a few Vietnamese families. Initially, she was put back a grade and given a tutor to learn English. Once she could speak English, she was put in her regular grade; she says she adapted easily. In fact, she was ahead of the Americans in math, which she found easy.

In 1977, Nga's parents moved to a large West Coast city where they took jobs in the electronics industry. "Now there were a lot more Vietnamese. We moved into low income housing; that's all we could afford." She went to middle school and then to high school in that city.

Many writers have commented on the closeness of Vietnamese families and the ways in which brothers and sisters take care of each other. Nga says that is not the way it was in her family. "We didn't spend a lot of time looking after our younger brothers and sisters. But each kid somehow got the message. We didn't need to be told; we knew the unspoken rule: 'Do well in school and don't mess around.' No dating was allowed, either in high school or in college. We never sat down and talked about it, but we followed literally the rule we all understood: 'Dating is for when you are done with school; don't get into a relationship in school.'" In high school she had a curfew, and it remained in force even when she returned home after college. She married a couple of years after she had completed her university studies. In mid-1995, she was expecting her first child.

Caplan, Choy, and Whitmore emphasize that successful families are those where parents oversee children's homework and determine the school subjects and careers of their children. This did not happen in Nga's family. The encouragement she received was more subtle. "When I was in high school, I played on the volleyball team for three years. My grades were above average, about a B, but I did not excel in any area. I did not know or think about college. I received no expectations from home; neither did my brothers and sisters. My parents were satisfied with my grades, but they gave me no guidance. They trusted me to know what I was doing. They did not claim to know more than me about what I should do. They expected me not to drop out or to do riff-raff."

After high school, Nga attended two community colleges for one year each. During that time, she also worked for a major computer company and also played on the volleyball team. She intended to go into chemical engineering, but she found that jobs were scarce, so she switched to electrical engineering, where jobs were plentiful. She explained her decision, "I'm very methodical. I look into it. I do things for a reason. I went into electrical engineering for the security it brings, not because of interest. I took tests, and they said with my personality I should be an engineer. I'm logical. I go with numbers and statistics, not intuition."

Nga transferred to a four year university about 150 miles from her home. She knew that her parents would not want her to go to a university further away than that. "I never met with them formally; we talked informally. I didn't say I insist on choosing my major but rather let them know what I was studying. They were happy with my choice and didn't say no. For me to move away from home was a big thing, but here, too, there was no resistance from them. I became a model for them to point to, and a role model for my younger brothers and sisters."

Of her university years, she said, "I fit in perfectly. I had a lot of Vietnamese friends, female and male (not romantic), and I became involved with our Vietnamese Student Association, which some charitable work and more cultural and social activities. I didn't know anything about organization, but I learned through that group, and I had a lot of fun with it."

In her electrical engineering class of 200, there were ten Asian females; five were Vietnamese. Nga did well in her studies, and she explains why, "You don't need to be real smart to do well. If you have average intelligence but have the effort, a positive attitude, the discipline, and the desire, you can succeed. To excel, you need discipline. I tried hard. I gave it an above average effort, and I did well. I am not smart. I believe, your effort determines how high you can go."

Mr. Le Van Hieu, a first wave refugee now in his early thirties, came to the United States with his family at the age of 13. He has not lived up to his own or his parents' expectations for schooling and career, though in recent years he has done well. Hieu clearly states what his parents expected and demanded from him.

> After graduating from high school, I went to the local public university. My parents told me to go there because it was the closest to my home. They didn't want me going far away. Many Vietnamese parents are like that. Some of us children think that they are too conservative, that we should be able to make our own choices. Our parents make other decisions for us: the classes we should take, our academic majors, even our schedules. Until the age of 21, I had a curfew. I had to be back home at midnight. What they want from us is to study, to concentrate on education, and not to take drugs or alcohol. They don't want us even to take a job. They would rather work overtime to let us study more. Our job is to get an education.

> During my first couple of years at the university, I did not focus on my studies. I'd cut classes. I was not doing well. The year was 1982 and the economy was down. Our family had just bought their house, and their income was tight. Dad was worried about me. One day, he sat me down and

asked, "What about your future? What will you do with your life?" Well, I had been feeling bad about this already. Here I was the oldest kid in the family, lacking discipline, doing poorly in school, contributing nothing, and setting a bad example for my younger siblings. Unknown to him, I had enlisted in the Army, thinking it might give me the discipline I needed, and also training for a better job. So I said, "Well, Dad, I'll be going into the Army in about two weeks."

He was stunned. After a moment, he said, "Okay, Son, joining the military probably will be good for you. It will give you the discipline you need." He wasn't worried because the U.S. wasn't in a war at that time. Mom took it much harder. I could see the shock and disbelief on her face. Her first question was, "Can you get out of it?" I replied, "No, Mom, once you sign the contract, you're in." Then she accepted it, though both she and Dad were disappointed.

I liked the military. It made me more responsible. I realized that what my parents had told me was true, and I understood why they said it. When I had to clean the bathrooms, I realized that without education, that's what I would end up doing. I learned to appreciate what I had and that I had not taken full advantage of it before.

Hieu decided not to reinlist because his father had been laid off from his job and soon after suffered a stroke. To remain in the Army would mean moving around a lot and being separated from his family. Hieu returned home with a different attitude. His parents also had changed. "I did not want to get back into the same bad habits, so I went to a college 200 miles away. Now that I was older, I picked my own degree, information systems management. After I had gone into the military, it had opened up my parents' eyes. They were no longer so very strict. They changed, both towards me and my younger brothers and sisters." Two of them went to private colleges and two attended universities in other cities. One sister is an engineer, a brother with a business degree opened up a small company, another is a computer engineer, and the youngest, with two years of college completed, plans to go into business or medicine. Hieu is now employed and in 1995, he married a Vietnamese American woman.

Nga and Hieu had the good fortune to live in families in which there was parental guidance and control, either direct or indirect. Such was not the case for Do Phuong Vi, born in central Vietnam in 1977, and her brother Quang, who is one year older. In Vietnam, they lived with their parents and two younger siblings. The family was desperately poor, though apparently stable. At the ages of 11 and 12, their parents sent them out of Vietnam alone, telling them that they would have a better future elsewhere. Vi wanted to leave but her brother did not. They landed in Hong Kong and for two years were moved into and out of five detention centers, overcrowded, steel-encased hotbeds of violence, degradation, and social disruption. Vi recalls those days, "During that time, I had no schooling. The Hong Kong camps were horrible. I remember riots and killing, boredom and loneliness." Then they were transferred to a transit camp in the Philippines while they awaited resettlement in the United States. Here, too they received no schooling or parental guidance. This camp was even worse than those in Hong Kong. Vi explained, "I lived in constant fear of being beaten, kidnapped, and raped by the guards or by the people of the area. For an entire year, I did not venture out after 6 P.M. I don't want to think about those camps."

In America, because they were unaccompanied minors, they were placed in a foster home. Quang, however, soon got himself in trouble, and he and his sister had to move to another foster home, and then a third. Quang became involved with a Vietnamese gang. He was in a car when there was a shooting, and he ended up in juvenile detention. The authorities recognized that Quang, a lonely target who could easily be manipulated, had not been directly involved in the shooting. They knew that he was not yet a hard core gang member and that he felt sorry and scared about what had happened. The authorities offered to release him if he provided information about the gang. Since his life would then be in danger, they sent him and his sister to their aunt, who had recently arrived in the United States and lived in a town far removed from Vietnamese gangs. It was a place where the two youths had a chance to start over.

I spoke with Vi and Quang in January, 1993, one and a half years after they had come to the United States, when they were living in a foster home. In March, 1995, I spoke with Vi a second time, five days before she and her brother left for their aunt's house. In the first interview, Vi, though younger, did most of the talking because her English was better. She had been placed in a higher level math class than her brother. She was doing fairly well in school, even though she found it difficult. Her brother was having a harder time adjusting in school and in their foster home.

When you consider what was done to Vi and Quang, as well as other refugee children, the wonder is not that many drop out of school, but that any stay in. Vi said, "When I came to America, I was placed in the eighth grade, even though I had missed three years of school and had completed only the fourth grade in Vietnam. I felt old and stupid. I didn't know anything or understand what the teachers said. I tried really hard, but it did no good. I couldn't speak; I couldn't communicate. The teachers did not like me because I was shy and could not speak to them. They acted like I ought to understand them, but I couldn't. I felt so bad, because a person cannot live without communication. I wanted to go back to Hong Kong, even though there was no hope or future there."

Vi found herself in a hostile and destructive social environment that upset her personally, interfered with her studying, and affected her grades. "People in America were not friendly, including the Vietnamese who had come earlier. They did not want to mix with new arrivals. So I felt sad." She began to associate with gang youths, though she never fully went along with them. "I found that kids only cared for me if I was cool. To be cool, you have to wear nice clothes—no one cares how you get them—and some girls turn to shoplifting. Or you have to hang out all night with the guys, and then sleep with this guy or that, or smoke what they give you. They tell you to steal. And when you don't do what they want, they hit you, or drop you, or call you bitch. I don't want to be cool. I don't want to be manipulated."

By the following year, Quang was at a juvenile ranch and Vi, her grades plummeting, had been moved to a different foster home where she was receiving no parental guidance. Indeed, she had received none since she had left Vietnam six years earlier when she was 11. She described her life. "I eat out most of the time, at fast food places. I like America. In Vietnam, my parents told me what to do and controlled me. Here in America, I am free. I can come and go any time of the day or night. I like that."

Vi lives in a low-income neighborhood of a city dominated by Mexican American and Vietnamese gangs. In dress, mannerisms, body language, speech, and values, she and her older brother have taken on the culture in which they have found themselves. She now has a steady boy friend, also a Vietnamese unaccompanied minor with whom she can share her loneliness. But they live right on the edge of delinquency. "Last year, a friend of my boy friend gave me a lift; he had borrowed my boy friend's car. The police stopped us, searched the car and found a gun, so they handcuffed us and said we had to tell whose gun it was or they'd book us. I was really scared. When the high school found out, they threw us out. My boyfriend felt sorry about messing up my school; his friend hadn't told him about the gun. Now I go to another high school."

Vi's account of her new high school gives a depressing picture of student-teacher relations. "Some teachers are nice, but many are mean, like my history teacher. He gives us homework but doesn't ask if we understand. 'Write one page: did England have the right to regulate commerce in the American colonies?' I have a hard time; I don't know what this means. When I ask, the teacher says, 'What have you been doing in school? Read the book.' But I have read it, all 300 pages, and the answer is not in there. I want to learn, but I don't understand. I don't see how the reading connects with the assignment. The teacher has no time to see students; he has two jobs. So I ask my friends for help; all are Vietnamese boys."

Vi's only ties are to her older brother and to her boy friend. She expresses no interest in or concern about her family in Vietnam. But she is concerned about her brother. "He cares about me a lot, and he respects me. And I care for him. He's not a strong character; his friends made him get in trouble. I worry about him. And he worries about me. He calls and checks to see how I am doing." Concerning her boy friend, she says, "He and I don't have parents in America. I live in a foster home and he lives with a relative. I will be moving to another town. When he's old enough he plans to move to that town to be with me. As for the future, I don't know. I want to get out of high school and be with my boy friend. All I know is, I can take care of myself."

Vi and Quang began life in a stable, if impoverished, rural family in Vietnam. When in 1988 they left their country, their lives were utterly disrupted, first in the refugee camps and later on in American foster homes and the larger social environment in which they found themselves. When you consider what they had to endure, the loneliness, the abandonment, the fear and the helplessness, and the obstacles placed before them in school, it is no surprise that Quang took up with the juvenile gang that accepted him and made him part of their family. Vi's adjustments, choices, and outlook make plenty of sense; she made the best of what she saw available to her.

Not all unaccompanied minors fail. Quite a few have adjusted well in America, excelled in school, and have become successful in their careers. Many tell me that their obligation to parents or siblings in Vietnam motivates them to succeed in America. Vietnamese tell me that children do poorly when their parents pay little attention to them, focusing instead on acquiring material things. Some parents say that strict discipline at home leads to the success of their children in school; others say that excessive discipline alienates their children and discourages them from doing well. Success in school might be more likely where, as Zhou and Blankston have suggested, family and community bonds and obligations remain strong but also where parents, while exerting control and direction, are flexible in dealing with education, career directions, and social behavior.

6

Families in Transition

THE TRADITIONAL FAMILY

The 12-year old girl led the toddler into the room where I was sitting. "Say hello to Father's Elder Brother," the girl said, as she took the toddler's arms and placed them across her chest in a traditional gesture of respect. Then the older girl pushed the two-year-old's head and torso forward and down; she was being taught to bow. "Hello Father's Elder Brother," whispered the toddler. "Very good," I replied, complimenting the child on her respectful behavior. After that, whenever the toddler saw me, even if she were running past, she would stop, cross her arms, bow deeply, and greet me.

We were in Vietnam, in a house where I stay when I visit Ho Chi Minh City. The toddler had begun to learn about the basic values of submission, obedience, and respect for family members and elders that all Vietnamese are expected to know and follow.

In the past century, the Vietnamese family and society have undergone great changes (Liljestrom and Tuong 1991). Overseas communities such as those in the United States, have experienced even greater transformations, especially in gender relations and in the relationships between generations. Females have greater social and economic independence in America, in part because of their widespread participation in the job market. Vietnamese children who arrive in the United States soon stop bowing to elders as they acquire some of the values and behaviors of their American peers. Nevertheless, in one way or another, the core family values the little girl was learning are still widely taught in Vietnamese households the world over.

Older Vietnamese Americans, especially males, often idealize the traditional family as they remember it from their childhood. What they express are values based on the patriarchal Chinese family model, which has influenced Vietnam over the centuries. This ideal family is large, extended, hierarchical, patriarchal, and patrilineal, that is, descent is reckoned on the father's side. The family includes not only those who are alive, but deceased family members, who are venerated. A person's identity, obligations, and support come from the family. It is the family that typically influences the course of a person's life, from spouses selected to the occupations that a person holds. Indeed, both Woodside and Jamieson call the family the model for the organization of Vietnamese society. Many Vietnamese describe themselves and their culture as both orderly and emotional, and they see the family as representing this combination. On one side, the father represents discipline and authority, one who must be obeyed. On the other side, the mother represents nurturing and affection, the sentimental aspect of Vietnamese culture. Despite great changes in the Vietnamese family in America, traces of these elements are still evident. The family is the central institution of their lives. Steven Gold describes it as "the most basic, enduring, and self-consciously acknowledged form of national culture among refugees" But he also notes that women are not as enthusiastic about the patriarchal emphasis in the Vietnamese family as the men (Gold 1992: 54, 66). The values these women express may come, not from modern changes alone, but also from ancient Vietnamese traditions that have given a higher place to women than is found in the Chinese family model.

Phuong Hoang, the elderly central Vietnamese refugee who escaped with his family to the Philippines before coming to America, recalls that the children of the house were expected to obey and respect their parents and their teachers. "We grew up hearing proverbs that reminded us of our obligations: 'Fish without salt smells bad; children who talk back become bad.' To remember the role of our parents, we heard, 'When drinking water, remember its source.' When we become successful, we should remember our parents, who made that success possible" (Freeman 1989: 76-77). Other proverbs highlight the ideals of obedience and submission, not only to parents, but to other superiors. "When we love our children, we give them a beating; when we hate our children, we give them sweet words." Harsh discipline is the way that parents and teachers are expected to show love to children. Older Vietnamese believe that failure to discipline leads to unruly children. An elderly peasant woman recalls a proverb for females, "A dress cannot be worn over the head." She interprets this to mean that children should not argue with their parents over what is correct but must listen to them (Freeman 1989: 65).

The Vietnamese traditional family stresses disciplined authority of and obligation to the father, but also nurturance, sentiment, and affection, associated with the mother. An important family value is moral debt, the deep unpayable obligation that children owe parents for bringing them into the world and for the sacrifices and unconditional love that parents give their children. These values of the Vietnamese family have been deeply influenced by Confucian thought, coming from China. A central Confucian idea is the cultivation of virtuous conduct, which should develop the superior or ideal man. Virtuous conduct is found in the five relationships: ruler-subject, father-son, husband-wife, elder brother-younger brother, and friend-friend. Significantly, three of these focus on the family. The proper relationship of son to father is filial piety, that is, obedience, submissiveness, honor, and respect to parents. A child must also care for them when they are old (Henken and Nguyen 1981: 14; Marr 1981: 58; Woodside 1971: 11, 37-38).

The relationship between older and younger brothers is also key. The older brother is supposed to "teach, nurture, and protect his younger brother," in return for which the younger brother should be "self-denying and docile." As Jamieson observes, "Unlike most Western children, children growing up in traditional Vietnamese families learned dependence and nurturance, not independence. They learned the importance of hierarchy, not equality. They learned the rewards of submission to those of senior status, not assertiveness." This is reinforced, not only in the expected behavior of older and younger brothers, but also in folklore, in which the meek and submissive, rather than the assertive, succeed (Jamieson 1993: 16-18; Freeman 1989: 27-107).

Studies of the third family relationship, between husbands and wives, reveal a conflict between the Chinese Confucian teachings which were imposed on the Vietnamese for 1000 years and the indigenous traditions which preceded Chinese rule. Vietnamese gender roles depart somewhat from the ideal Confucian view. In the ideal Confucian family, "women were supposed to be submissive, supportive, compliant toward their husbands. Husbands were supposed to teach and control their wives as they did their younger brothers and their children" (Jamieson 1993: 18). A traditional female should exemplify the principle of chastity, purity, and absolute faithfulness to her husband. She should follow the three submissions: she should obey her father when she is a child, her husband when she is married, and her oldest son when she is a widow. Beyond that, she is expected to achieve the four virtues of a woman: good cooking or sewing and housework, good appearance (for one's husband), careful or appropriate speech (self-demeaning and polite), and proper or good conduct (honest or loyal to one's superiors) (Henken and Nguyen 1981: 14; Marr 1981: 192-199).

A middle aged boat person who came to the United States in 1980, recalls how her father taught her morals and proper behavior at dinnertime. "All of us children feared him," she said. "First we were supposed to invite our relatives, and this had to be done with proper respect. We had to eat properly with chopsticks, and slowly, not fast. We had to speak properly, as girls should do. And if we made a mistake, he would shout out, 'Ho! Attention! No more!' I feared him."

Proverbs support the subordination of females and describe how a bride should be selected: A refugee recited to me, "When you buy a pig, choose the sow. When you buy a girl, choose the generations." He also said, "If a bride is doc-

ile, she is feminine; if a groom is pious, h
man 1989: 45). Other well-known pro
reinforce women's subordinate position.
angry, refrain from talking back. Boiling
when you lower the flame." "A hundred
worth a single testicle" (Marr 1981: 193).

But this view of women does not accura   ...ect Vietnamese social reality or actual women's roles, past or present.
The discrepancy between the ideal and the actual state of affairs has been a source of tension in Vietnamese society, as
well as disagreement among those who write about the family, and this tension has increased in the Vietnamese American family. Woodside writes, "Respect for the rights and
powers of women had always been more the mark of Vietnamese social conventions than of Chinese" (Woodside 1971:
44-50). Jamieson explains why: "Vietnamese myth, legend,
and history are filled with stories of strong, intelligent, and
decisive women. In all but the uppermost strata of society,
men and women often worked side by side. Women performed many arduous physical tasks, ran small businesses,
and were skilled artisans"(Jamieson 1993:18).

Another study of North Vietnamese farming families
paints a different picture, portraying women as money managers in many families and often controlling the money of the
household, which was locked and stored in a wooden trunk.
A popular saying is based on this custom, "The wife holds the
key to the trunk" (Nguyen Tu Chi 1991: 75). In rice cultivation, Nguyen Tu Chi stresses, women participated on an
equal basis with men. "In agriculture women are not regarded as helpers to men. They are considered equal to them.
There is no wonder, then, that the husband and head of the
household has no absolute power over the use of the harvest-
ed rice. Apart from the daily domestic needs, the head of the
family must have the consent of his wife when he wants to
take a quantity of rice from the rice container. If after long discussions, the wife does not agree with him, the husband must
give up"(Nguyen Tu Chi 1991: 74).

Accounts of village life differ on the extent of women's
authority. One study of two villages found that although
women participated in family decision-making, husbands

ad the final say and typically controlled the household income, including large expenditures for housing, ceremonies, purchase of family furniture, and investment in production (Dang Nguyen Anh 1991: 189, 194).

CHANGES IN VIETNAM

The traditional Vietnamese family is said to be that found in north Vietnam, the center of Vietnamese culture. Over the centuries, it has undergone many changes. When, in the late 18th century, the Vietnamese moved into what is now south Vietnam, they encountered different ecological conditions that favored agriculture by smaller family units and looser connections of families to villages than are found in north Vietnam. Contacts with peoples such as the Cham, who had been influenced by India, also affected family rituals (Do Thai Dong 1991: 86-92).

The coming of the Europeans, urbanization, the disruptions of war, and post-war Communist social and economic reforms also have also altered the family. There have been "changes in generational structure, acceleration of the process of nuclearization of the rural family, a decrease in household size, a reduction in the fertility rates, an increase in the number of women working outside the family, and an improvement of social education." (Do Thai Dong 1991:93).

These changes are especially marked in urban areas. As cities grew in the 19th century, a new type of family appeared among government employees, in which the husband was the provider and the wife took care of the house. Unlike rural families, in which women had an economic function, these new urban families strengthened the economic dependency of women and the husband's patriarchal power. Other changes also occurred: young people "demanded their right to choose their mates and marry out of love. Most of the urban families allowed their daughters to go to school," usually up through the secondary level, though few were allowed to obtain even low level clerical employment. With the 1945 August Revolution of the Communists, the principle of the equality of females and males was emphasized, which questioned the values of the Confucian family. With the defeat of the French in 1954, the Communists in north Vietnam instituted agricultural and social reforms including the nationalization of land and the abolition of private ownership. In rural areas, these reforms led to the formation of nuclear families. Literacy campaigns in the villages were also aimed, in part, at improving the status of women. The Confucian family came under fire as a feudal institution which denied women equal rights. In the cities, increasing numbers of women took jobs in government offices (Khuat Thu Hong 1991: 198-202).

The years of war, first involving the French and later the Americans, greatly disrupted Vietnamese families. Several million men went to war and were absent from their families. Of these, 1.1 million Communist (North Vietnamese and National Liberation Front) soldiers and 600,000 South Vietnamese soldiers died; 2 million civilians were killed. The wives of these absent men had to earn money and run their own households.

The Communist victory in south Vietnam in 1975 brought still more changes in the family. First, Vietnam's economic crises, caused in part by its own economic and social reforms, reduced many families to extreme poverty. This put a great strain on economic cooperation among relatives. Second, the new regime instilled a climate of fear and distrust in which people worried that others, including their own children, might turn them in for saying or doing something that Communists did not like. Third, the families of the several hundred thousand men who were put in reeducation camps were faced with additional burdens. Since the prisoners were being starved, their families had to give them food and other materials to keep them alive. The families were considered and often treated as enemies because of their association with the defeated south Vietnamese regime; they were denied employment and their children were not allowed to complete higher levels of education (Freeman 1989: 199-287). In addition, some widows of these prisoners remarried; other wives did not wait for their husbands to return from the camps; they married again or began to live with other men. The children of the reeducation camp prisoners often found themselves unwanted by their stepfathers and stepmothers. They were mistreated, and in some cases thrown out of the house or sent away as boat people refugees. Many of these children are now in the United States. Miss That Thao, the unmarried counselor, singer, and photo lab worker, recalled with bitterness that her stepmother let her father die in a reeducation camp. By the time he died of malnutrition, hunger, and cold, all his teeth had fallen out and he weighed only 84 pounds. Miss That Thao's stepmother never wrote to her husband or sent him food or anything else. She said to her stepdaughter, "I don't care if he dies."

A fourth disruption was caused by the exodus of two million refugees, including people from north Vietnam. Families were separated in flight, during which many were killed; other families deliberately sent out husbands or sons, and sometimes daughters, hoping to give them a chance at a better life while the rest of family remained in Vietnam. A large number of the unaccompanied minors sent out were the unwanted stepchildren mentioned above, the casualties of families already disrupted by war and reeducation camps. A fifth change aimed at breaking up the traditional family by giving it no legal basis: "Socialist law has abolished all relations bound by law between individuals and their kin, and recognized the equal rights of all citizens before the Law....kinship no longer has the function as a community by law in the new regime" (Khuat Thu Hong 1991: 198-202). However, despite the vicissitudes it has faced, the traditional family continues, especially in the countryside. Hy V. Luong's recent anthropological study of a north Vietnamese village confirms this. "In Son-Duong, the rise of collectivism and the greater participation of women in the public domain notwithstanding, the male-centered hierarchy of the colonial and precolonial eras persisted both within the communal framework and the kinship system"(Luong 1992: 185).

CHALLENGES IN AMERICA

Writers frequently comment on changes that have occurred in the Vietnamese American family, as well as elements of tradition that have been retained. But we have seen that change did not begin in the United States. It had been occurring over several centuries as the Vietnamese adapted to, among other things, colonial rule, war, and Communist reforms. However, the Vietnamese family in America, transplanted to a new cultural and economic setting, faces serious challenges that it had never faced in Vietnam, even under the most disruptive of war conditions.

Many refugees came to the United States leaving some or all of their close family in Vietnam. For those who came by themselves, loneliness is a major problem. In the first couple of years after the Communists took over south Vietnam, it was impossible to find out what had happened to family members left behind, and this was a source of great stress for those in the United States. In later years, those who were without family here still had a hard time. A Buddhist nun told of her efforts to help refugees on their own: "Many young adults in the ages of 20-25 have no family in this country. They are very lonely. Often they come by themselves to the pagoda. I cook for them. I provide some family for them, like a sister figure. If they need something and I have the possibility, I help to show them that somebody cares about them, pays attention to them" (Freeman 1989: 397). When such people got bad news from Vietnam, that their relatives were hungry or died or were in a reeducation camp, they became particularly depressed. According to the nun, about ten people a month told her that they did not want to live. While old people felt particularly isolated and depressed in America, "they are not the ones who attempt to take their lives; mostly it is younger men and women in the middle twenties and early thirties, people who have no family and who have felt lonely; they have had no one with whom to talk....They have no support. Life has no meaning. Whether they die today or later makes no difference" (Freeman 1989: 400-401).

A Catholic nun observed similar problems. "In the last four to six weeks, ten people told me they wanted to commit suicide. Most were young men in their early twenties who needed a job, were lonely, and were frustrated. They had come to America with such high expectations; now they had nothing to eat. Of the ten young people who spoke to me of suicide, three actually made the attempt, including two sisters, alone in America, who had been a medical doctor and a pharmacist in Vietnam."

To be separated from family is to experience an acute sorrow. One man said to me, "On the outside, I am like an American. I drive to work in my car. I eat hamburgers at lunch. But on the inside, I am Vietnamese; I cannot forget my mother, hungry in Vietnam while I have it easy here" (Freeman 1989: 19). An unaccompanied minor, who fled Vietnam to avoid political persecution, expressed his deep loneliness by writing poetry. His poems, which follow traditional Vietnamese forms of meter and rhyming, have an extraordinary power and depth (Freeman 1989: 419-423). He spoke to me about how he felt at being separated from his family, "I am lonely; I live in a strange land, and I have no direction like I did in Vietnam. I have no friends, no family, no lover....When I think of how lonely I am in America, I wonder why I am here, what I have to live for. And my poems speak of my unhappiness" (Freeman 1989: 422).

Many people who came to the United States alone, take up residence with near and distant relatives who had arrived earlier. A boat person refugee described how he first joined a household that consisted of his aunt's family. He rented a room and helped with other expenses. His mother remained in Vietnam, and he corresponded with her regularly. He never felt comfortable in his aunt's house. After two years he moved into a house with friends. He remained there for several years until he married. It is not uncommon for single men to move several times, sharing accommodations with friends and relatives.

While intact families, especially large ones, find the cost of housing and health care a continual problem, the benefits of living in large immigrant and refugee families outweigh the disadvantages. By sharing resources, these families can survive conditions of scarce resources and unemployment. Nazli Kibria suggests that greater success is found in large families composed of members of different age and genders. This diversity allows access to a wider variety of institutions, agencies, and employers that might benefit them. Kibria is particularly interested in the ways in which Vietnamese families share not only income, but information, services, and education. As Gold observes, "Thousands of Southeast Asian refugees work in the underground economy while simultaneously collecting public assistance and other benefits" (Gold 1992: 150). Others in the household might be receiving refugee cash or medical assistance, or, when those terminate, they apply for additional benefits, such as Aid to Families with Dependent Children, Medicaid, food stamps, or General Assistance. In Kibria's view, not only is this economic aid significant for the survival of the families, but the relationships refugees form with officials and agency workers are also important sources of information about jobs, bank loans, and educational opportunities (Kibria 1993: 77-107).

GENDER

One of the major issues facing Vietnamese American families is changing gender roles. As a rule, in Vietnam men maintained a dominant position even though rural women worked alongside them, and urban women had begun to hold jobs outside the home. As Kibria has observed, however, often these jobs were sporadic, with women only turning to them when the family had special economic needs or crises. Still, because many refugee women had been engaged in wagework in Vietnam, the transition to the United States has been less disruptive than it might have been had the women never been employed.

In the United States, there has been an increasing trend towards equality of females and males. One reason has been the widespread movement of women into the American work force. In Vietnam, one or two males ordinarily could earn enough money to maintain a large extended family; not so in America. Here, women must be employed to survive; the incomes they earn give them an independence they did not have in Vietnam. They develop new kinds of relationships outside the house, with employers, government agencies, and even schools. At work, they meet males socially and have greater freedom in interacting with them than was the case in Vietnam. Even those who work at home may develop greater independence because of the incomes they earn (Kibria 1993: 141). Gold observes that a major concern for young single men is that, with a shortage of Vietnamese women in the United States, the women are choosy; the men claim that the women look for money, not love, though the women themselves deny that (Gold 1992: 123).

The workplace not only opens up new possibilities for change in family and gender relations, it sometimes requires it. Vietnamese meat packers in Garden City, Kansas, have had to change their family life and gender roles to conform to the organization of work and employer policies. Mothers traditionally were viewed as nurturers who spent a lot of time with their children. Central to their role was the careful and time-consuming preparation of meals. Benson notes that female meat packers drop these activities."When a mother goes to work, the diet may suddenly change from nutritious Vietnamese meals to high-sodium packaged noodles or American 'fast foods.'"Fathers as well as mothers take care of children. This, too, is nontraditional. When parents aren't around, children get themselves ready to go to school. Child care may be managed by a parent when not on the work shift, by a relative, an unemployed member of the household, slightly older siblings, or low cost, unlicensed women who work as baby sitters. The care of children becomes not only haphazard, but sometimes dangerous for the children, who become "subordinated to the requirements of work." If they are fired or cannot find employment, the families move, even if this disrupts the schooling of children, "because the family must support itself." (Benson 1994: 99-126).

Many women have arrived in the United States without their husbands, who for various reasons were left behind, some failing in attempting to escape, others incarcerated in reeducation camps. After several years in America, the women have become much more independent and have modified their behaviors and beliefs. When their husbands arrive, the women are in a position of superiority; they are employed, while the men are not; they speak English, while the men frequently cannot; they are familiar with American customs, about which the men are ignorant. And the women are unwilling to return to the old ways.

A refugee in her forties says, "My parents chose a man for me whom I did not really want. I thought that all men were good because my brothers were good. Now I know that not all men are like that. I am very sentimental and emotional. I wanted to marry a teacher or a doctor, a man who would be gentle, educated, and cultured. I love art and music. Instead, I married a military man, and he wasn't gentle. I wasn't happy, but in those days, it wasn't like the United States; you couldn't get a divorce. So I had to endure and suffer for many years. He never helped me with anything; he never took care of his children, and he never gave me any money. I feared him because he would bully me. That's the way Vietnamese men are, they are bullies. American men are not like that."

In 1980, this woman and her children escaped to America. She left her husband in Vietnam and was reluctant to sponsor him to come to America. She speaks no English. She earns a small income designing and making dresses. She says, "I like American ways and American people; I like the freedom that women have here." She does not want to be controlled by Vietnamese men.

Miss That Thao, who has remained single, expresses similar attitudes. "I like Americans, they are helpful, generous, and nice. They are talkative and expressive. The Vietnamese men are always silent. I see a lot of Vietnamese women abused by men. I don't like that. The husbands control their lives and abuse them, hit them, hurt them, prohibit them from doing anything. But when the husbands cheat on their wives, they have no right to do anything. It's not fair. We all have a right to improve and be the best. Many Vietnamese men are insecure and don't want to see women progress. I would not be comfortable marrying a Vietnamese man; they are too controlling. I'm looking for a man who is nice, generous, open, and open minded. I don't find Vietnamese men like that."

There are still many refugee women who express more traditional attitudes. Mrs. That, who is 80 years old, defers to and serves her husband. She speaks no English; she remains at home where she cooks Vietnamese meals, raises vegetables, and sometimes talks to friends on the telephone. She wears the traditional village-style black trousers and white shirt. "I cannot eat American food. No hamburgers. I cannot eat butter or cheese, not even beef, ham, or milk....Here in

America, I just remain. I don't change my traditional ways; I still keep them....most Vietnamese women in the U.S.A. will become men [dress like men]....they dress according to what the people here do, except older women like me, who keep our old ways. The older women don't change much, and most of the older men don't change either"(Freeman 1989: 372, 273).

The wife of Colonel Tran Dinh Bui, 60, also serves her husband, but at the same time, wears American-style trousers and shirts. In Vietnam, she had remained at home; she has engaged in wage work for nearly all of the 20 years that she has been in the United States. She represents a pattern among women that Kibria says is widespread: they continue as wage earners, but support the traditional family. It gives them power as mothers over children. Indeed, refugee women see maternal authority and power threatened in U.S. society (Kibria 1993: 132-143).

Mrs. Quynh Nga, the electrical engineer, has just turned 30. She also exemplifies how Vietnamese women take on increased power in the family relative to men while at the same trying to preserve the traditional family system. Nga blends modern employment in America with Vietnamese family values and behaviors. During college, she did not date. After she completed her degree, she dated, but not much. "I wanted to be attracted to a man; otherwise I would not date. I thought, if I date, I must marry. I didn't think I'd play the field but rather if I liked someone, I'd commit to that person and marry him, and that's what I did." She and her parents expected her to marry a Vietnamese man. They told her she could marry whomever she loved, but they really wanted her to marry a Vietnamese man. "To marry an American would be difficult. To make it work, you have to adjust a lot. That's why everyone in my family has married a Vietnamese."

Nga commented that her job was not a traditional one for Vietnamese women. "In Vietnam, there were a few teachers, professors, and lawyers; the more traditional women were homemakers. Here in America, I live in two worlds. Outside the house, I am more American, a modern day woman, an educated and professional woman. But I still have a role as a homemaker. So I don't have to build up a career and have my career come first. I expect to raise a family. My career is second to my family. And I want to rear children as my parents reared me, except for some changes. My husband and I didn't have a lot of interaction between our parents and ourselves. I think there should be more. I was one of seven children. My parents didn't know me on an individual basis. I would like to have more communication with my children."

When Nga's husband came in the room during the interview, he said, "Both parents should have the same ideas regarding children. Vietnamese parents are too distant; we won't be like that. We expect to exert discipline, but to be more flexible than our parents were. You have to be at the kid's level. You have to know how they think and be flexible, not rigid." Nga concluded, "We'll be flexible and do things and raise the children together, but still, I'm more Vietnamese than American. I want to see respect for elders, respect for education, and an appreciation for what you have. It doesn't have to be a lot, just enough to be comfortable."

Kibria has described the uneasiness of many Vietnamese men regarding changing gender relations in America. Of the men whom I talked with, the older ones were the most disturbed by what they saw. Younger men often spoke about marrying women who would be their friends and equals, though not in everything.

Mr. Le Van Hieu, who described how he joined the Army, talked about how he viewed marriage and Vietnamese women. "My parents are very liberal; they are not restricted to tradition. They might like to introduce me to a possible wife, but they will not select my wife for me, nor force or pressure me to marry her. I am the eldest son, so my parents have expectations for me. I set the standard for my sister and younger brothers. Even so, my parents have been open minded and understanding. They have told us that whoever we meet and love, that person should be our choice. We are Buddhists, but they say we can marry a person of any religion. Their only request is that we not follow our spouse's religion if we don't want to. We can marry a person who is non-Vietnamese as long as we are happy."

Hieu, however, combines both Vietnamese and American values. "I would expect to choose a wife who is agreeable to my parents. Her behavior is important. I wouldn't marry a person who is not acceptable to my parents. She must also show respect to my parents. For myself, I want a wife who is understanding, who loves me, and who is not only a wife but a friend. I don't expect her to stay at home, cook, and be a traditional wife. Her education is up to her, too, but she should be able to survive. If she wants to work, it's up to her. Ideally, I want to be the provider."

Hieu married a Vietnamese woman, and he explains why. "Every one of my relatives has married a Vietnamese, and I prefer that too. We understand each other better, have the same culture and speak the same language. We think the same, and we have the same nonverbal communication, the eye contact, the touching of one's hair. In public, the Vietnamese will hide their feelings and emotions; at home they will be more affectionate. I'm more adapted to American ways; I am not afraid to show affection.

Still, I want to keep the good traditions of the Vietnamese. I think the sense of order, hierarchy, and respect for the elderly is good. We speak using special words of respect to those who are older and who have higher rank. I also value family closeness. Unlike Americans, who are more individual, the Vietnamese put family ahead of self. I am family oriented. Though I can live on my own, at the age of 32 I still live with my parents. I help them out financially, give them emotional support, and help out in the house. I sacrifice my freedom and privacy to live with the family."

Mr. Ly Long, who at age 26 has started his own business, also prefers the behavior of Vietnamese women. He said, "I used to like American women. Then I changed my mind. My friend married a French woman. She cannot eat Vietnamese food. They are not one hundred percent compatible. I see that it's hard to be compatible with Americans. My parents say I can marry any woman if I am happy, but I know they would prefer a Vietnamese woman. So do I. They have the same traditions, culture, and language as us, even though I'm not very good at it myself. But in Vietnamese, we can talk more intimately than in English. A Vietnamese husband refers to his wife as younger sibling. When speaking to him, she also refers to herself as younger sibling. She calls him older brother.

When speaking to her, he also refers to himself as older brother. Those are intimate terms. But what does English have?
'Hey, you, get over here.' So I feel more close, more romantic
in Vietnamese."

GENERATIONS

If gender roles within families are changing in America, so,
too, are relations between the generations. One elderly refugee lamented, "In America, there is nothing to hold our family together. In this city alone, my family numbers some 16
people spanning three generations. We live in several loca-
tions in the city. We also have others of our family living
elsewhere in America. Even so, we have nothing to look forward to. If I returned to Vietnam, the Communists would
put me in a reeducation camp, which would kill me. But here
in America, my wife and I will die a lonely death, abandoned by our children"(Freeman 1989: 367-368).

With these words, Mr. Ngon, a first-wave refugee born in
1906, concluded his life history, which he narrated to me in
1984. Times have changed since Mr. Ngon uttered those de-
spairing words; the United States and Vietnam have reestablished diplomatic relations, 20,000 Vietnamese Americans
visit Vietnam each year, and most returnees no longer need
fear that they will be imprisoned. But Mr. Ngon, now 89 years
old, remains heartbroken over what he sees as the disintegration of his family. His sons and daughters have achieved
what many call the American dream. They are highly educated and successful professionals earning high incomes: they
include two medical doctors, two engineers, a commercial
airline pilot, and a certified public accountant. But as far as
Mr. Ngon and his wife are concerned, their children are failures because they no longer obey or show proper respect to
their parents.

Their relationships with their grandchildren are no better.
The youngsters do not speak Vietnamese and are unable to
communicate with their grandmother, who has never learned
English. Rarely do they use traditional forms of respect when
addressing their elders. They stand and sit in ways that do
not show respect. Though unintentional, their actions,

speech, and mannerisms offend their grandparents. Mr. Ngon speaks and is literate in Vietnamese, French and English. While in America, he has also learned Spanish so that he can speak to some of his neighbors. Because of his knowledge of English, Mr. Ngon and his wife have been spared the indignity and embarrassment faced by many elderly Vietnamese of having to depend on children or grandchildren to translate for them, or to interpret for them when they visit government offices or hospitals (see also Gold 1992: 125-126; Kibria: 1993: 151-153).

The views of Mr. Ngon and his wife are shared by most elderly Vietnamese in America, who are upset by what they see as the lack of discipline and respect, not only in the family, but in public behavior. An ethnic Chinese refugee from Vietnam remarks, "Americans are so careless about so many things. When they go out on the streets, they do not wear shirts, or dresses; some use the flag for shorts and for trousers. But the flag is symbolic of the country. Many people who stretch their legs on the bus don't leave room for other people...I see such disregard for people" (Freeman 1989: 412). Mr. Liem, a businessman who is half the age of Mr. Ngon, blames American law for the misbehavior of children. "In Vietnam, in educating our children, if we cannot get success telling them what to do, we would punish them with a beating....Here we cannot beat the children....There are so many Vietnamese teenagers who came to America and who became not good people because of American law. When parents beat the child, the police come and arrest the parent" (Freeman 1989: 387).

A number of elderly parents have come to the United States as ODP immigrants, sponsored by their adult children. Many become quickly disillusioned. They are not given respect, and they are not taken care of as they had expected. Their adult children are away at work; their grandchildren are in school; they remain alone, unable to speak English, afraid to venture out of the house to visit friends, go shopping, or visit churches or Buddhist pagodas.

Mrs. Tam, a retired schoolteacher who came to the United States in 1984, is one such person. Her husband had been murdered by the French during the French-Vietnamese conflict; she had reared and supported her children by herself since that time; she was an independent and active person. One of her adult children came to the United States and had sponsored her. But when she arrived in America, she found herself constrained and frustrated in ways she had not anticipated. She spoke French and Vietnamese; her grandchildren spoke only English. She could not go out and she had nothing to do. She contrasted this with her life in Vietnam. "Under the Communists, people like me who were over the working age of 60 could wander freely all about the town....It was easy for us to travel...we knew each other and visited each other. If I was sick, my friends visited me and I did the same for them. I would see my friends at the market. When I think of that, I miss not having people I know nearby" (Freeman 1989: 426). At the age of 76, after two years in her daughter's house, Mrs. Tam moved away to a city several hundred miles away. She has remained there ever since. She lives, not with relatives, but with several elderly friends. She feels more comfortable with them than with her own family.

Mrs. That, the elderly peasant woman, is also unhappy in America, but she is more typical in her responses. She does not speak English, so she is unable to fill out papers, answer the phone in English, or even to travel around, using public transportation as she did in Vietnam. She observes that in Vietnam, her children respected her, but not in America. "Here we need them more; they don't need us." Like many of the elderly Vietnamese in the United States, she pines to return to Vietnam to die. "If it were peaceful, I would live in Vietnam. I would live in the countryside because I have property and fields near the river, also a big garden with lots of fruits such as jackfruit and banana. I'd go back and live there. I'd make my living selling rice paper or chicken and pigs. It's more of a comfortable life" (Freeman 1989: 372, 373).

Many parents and grandparents see themselves as having sacrificed greatly to enable their children to have a better life in America, only to find that their children have abandoned them. They are devastated that their children distance themselves and disobey their authority. They blame American law, which interferes with traditional discipline; television, which offers new ideas to children; schools, which present alternative values and lifestyles that undermine parental authority; and economic opportunities in America, which enable children to be more independent, weakening parental control over children. A frequently cited complaint is that in Vietnam, society, school, and family presented similar values that reinforced one another. By contrast, in America, society and school undermine. Vietnamese family traditions (Kibria 1993: 146-149).

However, many of the children view this situation differently. Some, such as Mr. Le Van Hieu, are unable to live up to their parents' expectations for their education and employment. Even if they are successful in school and at work, they do not measure up to the social expectations of their parents. Many younger people wish they could have more open discussions with their parents and elder relatives, and many feel their parents are too rigid and strict.

Because he did poorly in high school, one young man's father punished him, but to no avail. "When I was in the 5th and the 7th grades, I wanted to participate in a walkathon for charity. My parents wouldn't let me. I wanted to join the cub scouts. They wouldn't let me. I missed out on that too. I didn't do too well in school. I didn't focus. I always had that problem, so I didn't concentrate. My grades were not good. I was more interested in sports, tennis. So I had a hard time in school. My parents didn't want me to play tennis. My father spanked me a lot. He punished me in ways that he didn't use with my older brothers and sisters. He'd tie my feet to a chair and people in the family would walk by. I didn't like it. He made me sit in the basement by myself for one to two hours. My relations with him went down because of his cruelty. By 10th grade my parents yelled at me a lot. They'd restrict me from doing stuff. I felt real bad. I tried to defy them, at least subconsciously. Dad worried about me. He thought I wouldn't graduate. But I did, with a B average. My parents went to my graduation. But my relations with my Dad remained strained. Later on, I went away to college, pulled myself together, and earned a degree in finance. I'm glad to have gotten it over, for myself and for my parents."

Many young people are concerned and frustrated that their fathers are unable or unwilling to openly express affection, as they believe Americans do, and some try to get their fathers to change. This may cause further strains. According to Nazli Kibria, cultural divergences of this sort have led to a loss in elders' ability to exercise authority over the young and have "also raised the prospect of the defection of the young from the collectivist household economy—a prospect that threatened the economic aspirations of family elders," who had "pinned their hopes for acceptance and prosperity in their adopted society on the future occupational attainments of the young" (Kibria 1993: 152-153).

CONTINUITY AND CHANGE

The chapters on employment, education, and family have documented the significant changes that Vietnamese Americans have experienced as they have adapted to the United States. In some areas they have faced conflicts with their traditional ways; in others they have made relatively easy transitions. In America, the more Westernized Vietnamese, with a long history of contact with the French and the Americans in Vietnam, were able to adjust relatively easily and served as brokers between other Vietnamese refugees and American society. A high proportion of Vietnamese refugees were Catholics who shared some values and traditions with other Americans. Much of the entrepreneurial success of the Vietnamese may be attributed to the large numbers of ethnic Chinese who came from Vietnam, bringing with them both a knowledge of and an interest in establishing businesses. The remarkable successes in school of many Vietnamese students also are partly attributable to their Vietnamese roots: the mandarin civil service exams plus one hundred years of French-imposed education. Finally, the Vietnamese family, while undergoing changes in America, often has provided a support system, as well as high motivation to succeed, not exclusively for oneself , but for relatives and the reputation of the family.

7

Changing Images of Vietnamese Americans: 1995

AMERICAN VIEWS OF THE VIETNAMESE

Twenty years ago, Americans knew little or nothing about the peoples of Vietnam, Cambodia, and Laos. Although the United States had been a major player in the Vietnam war, and dozens of books had been written about the war, Americans were largely ignorant of Vietnamese people and their traditions, and only a handful of Americans spoke any of the languages of that region. The war was described as an American war, with the Vietnamese little more than shadowy background figures and other Southeast Asians virtually non existent. There was a considerable literature about Vietnam by earlier French scholars, but for the most part Americans ignored it.

In 1975, when the refugees first began to arrive in the United States, Americans had virtually no information on how these newcomers might cope with life in the United States and view their new country. Several studies were done on the new refugees right at the time they arrived, and in the next ten years, additional accounts about the Vietnamese began to appear. At first many descriptions, especially popular accounts, focused on basic information on who the Vietnamese were, often with lists of their presumed cultural traits, family structure or personality characteristics as if these were somehow fixed and unchanging. The assumption was that if you understood the culture or knew the list of cultural traits, you would understand how the Vietnamese think and behave.

There were other problems with many of the early accounts of Vietnamese refugees. Following assimilationist assumptions, many focused on cultural traits that were seen as barriers to adjustment and assimilation, with middle class American values the yardstick for evaluation. Especially in the popular press, the Vietnamese were portrayed mainly as refugees from war, as boat people fleeing persecution, with little attention to any other aspects of their lives. Near the end of the first decade, popular accounts began to highlight Vietnamese success stories in education and employment. Vietnamese achievements were overplayed, while the problems they faced were underreported.

In the past decade, 1985-1995, a more complex view of Southeast Asian peoples has emerged in the writings of scholars (Camino and Krulfeld 1994; Ebihara, Mortland, and Ledgerwood 1994; Freeman 1989; Kibria 1993; and Welaratna 1993). There has been a movement away from a view of culture as a kind of basic, unchanging, and bounded entity. More and more, scholarly works emphasize that Vietnamese and other Indochinese traditions have always been dynamic and unchanging. The emphasis is on identity, not as fixed and unmoving but as fluid and flexible—as constantly being formed, recreated, manipulated and negotiated in different environments and circumstances. In general, research on recent immigrants now points to the great diversity and variety of adjustments among the Vietnamese and other groups, indicating that they are not simply victims of circumstances, but persons who creatively reconstruct their lives and their identities.

Contemporary studies demonstrate that change is not as simple as looking at assimilation to America or resistance to assimilation. Nor is it a straight line of before and after. Rather, change among immigrants is best conceived as is a complex process in which different groups and individuals, faced with different situations, creatively transform the worlds in which they live. The Vietnamese have not simply adjusted to America, but rather have made it their home. This is seen, not only in the occupations, schooling and training they choose, but in significantly altered family and gender relations, as well as transformed religious ways, which fit neither traditional nor American stereotypes.

During their first decade in the United States the top priority of the Vietnamese was simply to survive and recover from the refugee experience. Along with this, the refugees expressed vocal opposition to the Socialist Republic Vietnam, which they blamed for the refugee crisis. In the second decade, another phase of adjustments began, expansion from mere survival to economic strength and self-sufficiency. The hard line public opposition to Vietnam continued among refugees, particularly with regard to the reestablishment of diplomatic relations between America and Vietnam. Privately, though, a growing number of Vietnamese in America were sending money to their relatives, visiting Vietnam, and doing business in the land of their birth. Beyond the second decade, we can expect to see the Vietnamese developing new and distinctive ways of retaining or reconfiguring values and traditions in American social settings and strengthening their ties with Vietnam as their relatives resettle in America, not as refugees but as immigrants.

The Vietnamese experience started as a refugee saga, to which later was added an immigrant chapter. Now, after 20 years in America, although immigrants continue to arrive, the Vietnamese story is shifting to how they construct their identity as one group among many. This is occurring at a time when, as David Rieff has observed, Americans themselves, witnessing new immigration from Asia, are just becoming aware that "they now live in a genuinely multiracial country." The fundamental question, says Rieff, is "how people will conceive of themselves as Americans if the image of a country made up of blacks and people of European ancestry is only part of the story"(Rieff 1990: 543-544). That is precisely what the Vietnamese themselves are asking.

VIETNAMESE AMERICAN VOICES

In a prize-winning undergraduate essay, Minh Huynh, whose family came to America in 1975, writes, "If one were to ask a Vietnamese in Vietnam if I were Vietnamese, he or she would undoubtedly say no. The name used to describe a person such as myself would be *Viet Kieu*, which means foreign Vietnamese. If one were to ask a Caucasian in the United States if I were American, the answer would still be no. No matter how one views me, I am a Vietnamese American with a unique blend of both cultures. If I denied either my American or Vietnamese side, I would only be denying a part of myself. Like my family's guava tree [transplanted from Vietnam to America, giving the fruit a different flavor], I represent a new generation of Vietnamese and American that is not necessarily better, but different." The essay concludes, "Though my ethnic origin may be from Southeast Asia, my essence and soul is the conglomeration of all cultures. To describe me as either Asian or Asian-American would be grossly incomplete. I acknowledge Asian, Anglo, Hispanic and African influences to all be a part of my heritage "(Minh Huynh 1995: 7-8).

Minh Huynh raises two issues that are of concern to Vietnamese Americans and their families. One is that by adapting to America, Vietnamese traditions are threatened. Should one willingly endorse American values, thus abandoning tradition, typically associated with the family, or not? A second issue is the conflict between earlier arrivals, who have become Americanized, and newcomers as well as others who are less Americanized. The Americanized Vietnamese are referred to insultingly as "Bananas," with yellow skin on the outside but white American values and behaviors on the inside, people who have lost their roots and sold out their culture. Those who are less Americanized are called an equally derogatory term, *FOBs*, or Fresh off the Boat, people who cling to old ways and are likely to live in pockets of poverty unless they adapt to America. Minh Huynh observes that all people of Vietnamese descent in America have to choose between these extremes or somewhere in between.

The choices made by the Vietnamese and their ways of expressing them are quite varied:

"I am Vietnamese; I just live in America. I plan to go back to Vietnam, to my roots.(20 year old male)."

"I'm not a hyphenated anything. I am American. I just happen to have Vietnamese parents. I was born here, I speak English, not Vietnamese, and I value my independence. I'm not really interested in Vietnam; it's not my country.(24 year old female)."

"I am neither Vietnamese nor American. I don't fit in either group. I was born in Vietnam, spent several years in France, and now live in America. I am the mixture of three, not two cultures.(35 year old female)."

"I'm 30 percent American. I've been here 20 years. I came as a kid, so I know American ways. When I'm with Americans, I'm American, but at home I'm Vietnamese. I prefer Vietnamese values and the Vietnamese family.(Mr. Le Van Hieu)."

"I'm a typical Vietnamese woman. I care for my family and help my brothers and sisters in Vietnam. I like to do housework and cooking, although I work, too. Actually, I feel complicated, not Vietnamese, not American. The Vietnamese way is to accept your destiny, but I don't agree with that. I want to control my own life.(Miss That Thao)."

The Vietnamese are now talking and writing about themselves and their varied ways of negotiating between idealized Vietnamese and American values. Vietnamese identity is neither simple to define, nor unchanging, nor universally the same for everyone within the group. Their identities are derived from a wide array of experiences and cultural influences.

Vietnamese voices provide an important alternative to American views about them. The Vietnamese are writing both in Vietnamese and in English, and they are now critically evaluating both Vietnamese and American writers who deal with Vietnamese topics. Vietnamese American scholars and literary critics include some who came to America before 1975, such as Professors Huynh Sanh Thong and Nguyen Dinh Hoa, as well as many who came after the fall of Saigon.

Novelists, short story writers, and poets writing in Vietnamese who came to the United States in 1975 typically have written with nostalgia about the past in Vietnam, about guilt at having left behind relatives, friends, and others, about the betrayal of Vietnam by America, and their feelings of isolation in America. Qui-Phiet Tran comments on their reactions to American material civilization and moral values: "Vietnamese are appalled by American life, which they find too hectic, mechanical, competitive, and insecure." Americans do not appreciate "the value and benefits of human feelings....[they] do not highly value loyal friendship and matrimony, filial piety, and the like....Rather, they develop a cult of individualism and privacy, sometimes to the point of isolation".(Qui-Phiet Tran 1995: 46-47). A significant number of Vietnamese exile writers are females, whose images of exile and explorations of identity involve not only uprooting from the old, but an "imprisonment in obsolete, rigid, ethical principles."(Qui-Phiet Tran 1993: 77).

Writers who arrived as boat people, notes Qui-Phiet Tran, express little nostalgia for Vietnam. They have a "clear ideological purpose—to seek freedom and to tell the world about the 'Vietnam in blood and tears,'" a world of human misery and agony, "explaining the meaning of their unique ordeal to their fellow Americans." Significantly, in the writings of the boat people, attempts to escape are doomed to failure; just as they are about to reach the shores of freedom, they die. "Man in modern Vietnamese literature is condemned to an eternal inferno" (Qui-Phiet Tran 1995: 49).

Younger writers now explore themes of life in America; a growing number are writing in English. These include not only literary writers, but reporters and columnists at newspapers such as the Los Angeles Times and the San Jose Mercury, who describe and comment on a variety of issues in America, including the Vietnamese experience. In 1995, two young Vietnamese started *Vietnow*, which they term "the magazine about today's Vietnamese-Americans." Trendy articles in English, lavishly illustrated with photos, discuss Vietnamese American celebrities, films, arts and literature, repatriation, sex and relationships, identity, social issues, and fashion.

One of the most widely celebrated recent books is Jade Ngoc Quang Huynh's *South Wind Changing*, about the author's life, imprisonment, and escape from Vietnam, as well as a brief account of his first days in America. The book was the subject of a four page review in the **New York Review of Books** (Gourevitch 1994: 55-58). In sparse but powerful language, he recreates his experience of rejection in San Jose, California. He had taken his sister and "her frail skinny daughter" to apply for assistance at the Women, Infants and Children Program. He asked the receptionist for an appointment. "After speaking a few seconds, she put the phone down and looked at me sadly. 'The manager said she doesn't want any Vietnamese.' 'What?' I said, not believing my ears. The receptionist repeated what she had said very slowly, as if I hadn't understood. I was frustrated, insulted, and humiliated but didn't know what to do. I felt defeated. Sorry, niece, I thought, I cannot help you to receive a few free gallons of milk a month to help you grow. Why did I come here in the first place? I wished I could go home, to a place where at least my skin and culture, my morals and values were the same as others'. A place where I was born and spoke the language. I wished I could die there someday, coming back, to my roots, to the taste of the water and the air."(Jade Ngoc Quang Huynh 1994: 289-290).

FADING TRADITIONS

Given the momentous changes that have occurred in Vietnam over the past century, and the additional changes brought about in the different cultural environment of the United States, it is no surprise that the traditional ways often extolled by the elders are followed and understood by fewer and fewer Vietnamese Americans. Most older Vietnamese live in America with the memories of these old traditions. Mr. Phuong Hoang, the elderly boat person who escaped with his family to the Philippines in 1978, recalls with nostalgia his instruction as a child to train him to be a good citizen, to respect teachers and old people, as well as brothers and sisters.

"Ours was an education based on custom. We learned how citizens should pay taxes to the government, rules of politeness and respect, and the proper rules of relationship between young men and women, who should never touch or shake hands. If a man wanted to marry a particular woman, his parents should find an old friend or relative of the woman to serve as a matchmaker." He stated that both friends and spouses should be of the same social level, based first on character and moral reputation, second on education, and last on wealth. In his view, parents were the best judges of appropriate or inappropriate spouses for their children, and this was seen in a proverb, "A round lid fits a round pot, a misshapen lid fits a misshapen pot" (Freeman 1989: 78). He was unhappy in America because he saw these values and traditions being eroded.

Mr. An Thu, the 60-year-old high class ODP immigrant who came to the United States at the end of 1993, also discussed the old teachings in detail, while noting that they had changed greatly during his lifetime. His father, who was a mandarin official in the old bureaucracy, taught him Confucian values such as the five cardinal virtues and the principles of proper respectful behavior. He also learned from his mother. "When we were infants, she would chew the rice before feeding us; if we urinated on her only bamboo mat, she had to suffer, sleeping on it wet and cold, while letting us sleep in a dry area. In these ways, she showed us her love."

In the first twelve grades, he was taught a subject called the Education of the Responsibility of Citizens. "In elementary school, we learned to respect Father and Mother and how to treat older and younger brothers and sisters, friends, neighbors, and teachers, ancestors and grandparents, villagers and country. We learned from proverbs. One says that Father's deeds for the child are like the Thai Son Mountain, while Mother's devotion is forever, like the incessant spring at its source. Our brothers and sisters are like our arms and legs."

Other Vietnamese Americans, including some older people without much formal education, know little about Confucian traditions, have much less interest in them, and depart from them in various ways. Not surprisingly, those who came as youngsters are more *American* than *Vietnamese*. In an unsigned article, a first wave refugee college student expresses views that are held by many young people. "Having been raised in the United States for most of my life, I have no clear recollection whatsoever of the country in which I was born and have lost nearly all traces of my Vietnamese heritage.....Although my parents did share some of their knowledge of Vietnam and its culture with me, I feel that I am still culturally illiterate with regards to the Vietnamese culture. Since I never attended school in Vietnam, I missed out on learning classic Vietnamese literature, its indigenous traditions, and its history....My younger brother, sister, and I are more literate and well-versed in English than in Vietnamese....My brother, sister, and I never really had a life in Vietnam. We did not need to come to terms with anything, and we cannot regret anything. We just live"(Anonymous 1990: 7).

Teenage unaccompanied minors also may have little attachment to Vietnamese traditions. Do Phuong Vi and her brother Quang call themselves Vietnamese, but they know virtually nothing about the old Vietnamese traditions, and they express no interest in them. They define themselves as Vietnamese because that is how they are labeled at school, and because their friends are Vietnamese teenagers like themselves. Vi and Quang show little concern about their family in Vietnam. After three years in refugee camps and another three years in American foster homes, they have taken on the life style and values of American teenagers in a low income urban setting, as have their Vietnamese friends. Their memories of Vietnam have faded and are of less significance in defining their identities than are their American contacts.

VIETNAMESE AMERASIANS: NOWHERE TO GO; NOWHERE TO RETURN

Beginning in 1982, under the provisions of the Amerasian Immigration Act, Vietnamese Amerasians, children born in Vietnam of Vietnamese mothers and American fathers, were allowed to come to the United States, provided they had sponsors, but their mothers and other relatives were not permitted to resettle. In late 1982, under the ODP, Amerasians whose American fathers had filed papers for them were admitted to the United States; later, Amerasians without such firm documentation were brought in. Because of bureaucratic delays both by Vietnam and the United States, many children waited for years to be brought to the United States. In 1988, the Amerasian Homecoming Act paved the way to bring both Amerasian children and their immediate relatives to the United States, and through September, 1994, nearly 20,300 Amerasians and 56,700 of their relatives had emigrated to America. Most Amerasians do not know who their fathers are, and even if they do, they do not expect to be reunited with them. But they are coming to the United States anyway. Because American fathers were involved, and because of the advocacy efforts of people such as attorney Bruce Burns, the plight of Vietnamese Amerasians has received a great deal of attention.

Vietnamese Amerasians who come to the U.S. face an exceptionally difficult period of adjustment. Some report that, in Vietnam, they were mistreated or insulted and ridiculed at school by teachers or students who called them *half-Americans* or *half-breeds*. While many Amerasians were treated well most of the time, discrimination seems to have occurred most often if the child lived in an area controlled by Northerners or if the child's mother was considered to be lower class (Ranard and Gizlow 1989: 3-4; United States Catholic Conference, Marilyn Lacey 1985: 6-16). A number, however, were forced to become street children at the margins of society, scrounging for scraps of food. Many of these children were adopted by Vietnamese families and then mistreated. After passage of the Amerasian Immigration Act, adoptive families often used the Amerasian child to achieve immigration status. But once in the United States, these children were often abandoned.

One Amerasian youth, Tam Nguyen, described how, in Vietnam, his adoptive family yelled at him until he left them. He was 6 years old at the time. Twelve years later, they sought him out as their passport to America. He agreed to go with them to the United States. One day, he returned to the house they rented, only to find it empty and cleaned out; his adoptive family had disappeared. Abandoned Amerasians, many of whom speak little or no English, are deeply afraid of what the future holds. One said, "I don't have a future to talk about." Another says, "Life has always been hard, and now it will only get harder."

Compared with their Vietnamese peers, Amerasian children seem to be more likely to have difficulties in American schools. This is partly due to the fact that a higher percentage of Amerasians had little or no schooling in Vietnam, mainly due to poverty, which forced them to earn money rather than attend school (J. Felsman, Johnson, Leong, and I. Felsman 1989: 40-41) One the other hand, Mary Payne Nguyen, of the St. Anselm's Immigrant and Refugee Community Center in Garden Grove, California, who has helped many of these children, points to another factor. She says that Amerasians "have no peace of mind. How can they study, how can they concentrate after all they have gone through?" (Anh Do 1992: 1-2).

In addition to dealing with abandonment and mistreatment, Amerasians are often faced with acute identity problems. This is particularly evident in the case of Mr. Ngo Van Hai, a black Amerasian born in 1975. While he has had an easier time of it than those who were abandoned, his road has not been smooth. In Vietnam he was well treated by his adoptive parents. At the age of ten he was accidentally taken on a boat that fled Vietnam. After coming to the United States as an unaccompanied minor, he was placed in foster homes, encountered initial problems in adjusting, but finally responded to the guidance of his foster care social worker and a Caucasian foster family, who offered him both trust and firm discipline. He now attends college as a computer science major. While everything seems to be going well for him, he is very ambivalent about his own identity.

"On the outside I am black, but Vietnamese culture is trapped deep inside me. But I'm also glad I am an American. I prefer to be described as American. For some reason, when I went to college, I didn't want people to know I'm Vietnamese. I feel vulnerable. If I meet Vietnamese people, I don't mind them finding out I'm Vietnamese, but I prefer not telling them. When they know I'm Vietnamese, they accept me right away and are really friendly. They say, 'He can speak Vietnamese.' They accept me automatically. I would rather that they first find out something about me as a person, who I am. I'd like to see how they would treat me if I were not Vietnamese. If they treat me well, not knowing I'm Vietnamese, then I know for sure they are good."

RETURN TO VIETNAM

Amerasians are not the only ones who experience identity problems. Vietnamese Americans who return to visit Vietnam face a particularly trying challenge to their identity. Although they often idealize Vietnam and see themselves as Vietnamese, they find that they are viewed as outsiders by the Vietnamese who have remained in their country. The overseas Vietnamese also find that they differ in significant ways from their hosts. Nevertheless, by going back, some young Vietnamese Americans have reestablished connections with their ancestral villages, fulfilling their birthright and reaffirming the cultural roots that comprise their identities.

In 1994, Miss Thuan Le went back to visit Han Thien, a North Vietnamese village renowned for producing scholars and mandarin officials, and also the home of her maternal grandfather. Thuan had heard from her family in America about the beautiful city of Hanoi, the sparkling green rice fields, and the majestic mountain scenery surrounding the Huong Tich Mountain into which is built the legendary Chua Huong, or Perfume Pagoda, "a Mecca for Vietnamese Buddhists....the North's most famous shrine," but one her parents had never visited because of the war. Thuan visited Hanoi, which had deteriorated, compared to her grandparents' glowing descriptions. She noted, with concern, the large numbers of homeless people roaming the streets. She describes her visit to Chua Huong, where she climbed to the central shrine in a great cave high up on Huong Tich Mountain:

"I worked my way through the crowd to the main altar, closed my eyes and bowed to Buddha, in whom my family believes but whom I abandoned long ago. I didn't pray to the deity. I raised incense sticks to my forehead, smiled through smoke-caused tears and quietly told my ancestors: 'I made it. I pay respects on behalf of my father, who died three years ago, and my mother, who hopes to come soon.'" At Han Thien village, she found her ancestral home, which was run down and needing paint, divided into 50 tiny living units. The great trees that had once lined the walkway had long since been cut to make way for food stalls. She was unable to locate the graves of her ancestors but was shown a shrine with a red altar 12 feet high memorializing her ancestors. She was delighted to discover a framed list naming overseas relatives, including her grandmother, parents, and relatives, who had contributed to the upkeep of the shrine. "When I left, I was bitter that my family had lost our native land but happy that I had visited long-lost relatives" (Thuan Le 1994: E-1, 8-9).

Not all visitors respond as positively as Thuan. Miss Thu, who visited Vietnam the same year as Thuan, was deeply shocked by what she saw and experienced. Thu escaped from Vietnam in 1979 at the age of ten. Fifteen years later, she returned. "It never crossed my mind to go back, but a friend of mine who was traveling to Vietnam for six weeks asked me to accompany her, so I did. It was to be my dream vacation. I love photography, and I believed that Vietnam would be the place for me to explore my hobby. It turned out to be my vacation in hell. Saigon was really hot, dusty, and suffocating. My travel agent in Saigon took us in a four-door vehicle to the house of my friend's parents. The houses looked like they had never been repaired. When I was sent to our room, I looked around and saw something scurrying across the floor. I screamed. It was just a lizard. The next day, I went outside. The men stared at us. I was wearing shorts. One guy called out, 'Real pretty!' The men looked at me as if I were naked. A relative took me by motorcycle to a village. The people were friendly and asked me about America and Vietnamese singers in the United States. I tried not to speak English. They offered us food. We sat on the floor and I shared my meal with flies."

Later, she traveled around Vietnam. She found the experience unpleasant. "Beggars bothered us everywhere to such an extent that I could not enjoy the sights. The Vietnamese charge two prices, one for the Vietnamese and a higher price for overseas Vietnamese. I didn't like that. I tried to pass as a Vietnamese by wearing slippers and local clothes, but I fooled no one. Finally I visited my ancestral home. I remembered it as big. Now the patio and the gate were gone, the trees were dead, and the paint was faded. It was dirty. When I saw the house, I just felt empty."

Thu felt out of place; she looked out of place. Although she had tried hard to blend in, the Vietnamese continued to stare at her as a stranger. "By the fifth week of our trip, I had had enough. I counted the days until I left. At first I had thought I might like to go back to work or to help people. Now I wouldn't think of it. I can't handle the life style, the heat, the poverty, the food for which I had no appetite, the toilet in the back, and the smells. I always considered myself Vietnamese; at home in the United States, we speak Vietnamese, though with a mixture of English. But now I realize I have American values. I have been educated in America. When I saw Americans fighting about protection of the environment, I thought it was silly. But after seeing the Vietnamese scatter garbage everywhere, I feel different about it. When we were on the train, the Vietnamese tossed trash out the window onto the green mountains. We found this disturbing. We put our trash in a plastic bag and handed it to the conductor; he threw it out of the train. The Vietnamese live for themselves, not for society, the environment, or the future. They are too busy making a living to care about anything else. I cannot live in Vietnam. I don't like the fact that girls are supposed to stay home and are not allowed to do anything that is supposed to be 'men's business,' such as thinking. I like the Vietnamese respect for elders, but I dislike the seclusion of women. I used to think I'd only marry a Vietnamese guy, but not any more. I could marry a white guy now. I want a husband who appreciates things like the environment and doing community work. I don't find that in most Vietnamese men."

Miss Duong Thi Chi, a boat person who came to America as a 15-year-old in 1980, also described herself as very disappointed with Vietnam. I spoke with her when she was visiting Vietnam. Her remarks reveal the gap in values, attitudes, and behaviors between overseas Vietnamese and those who have remained in Vietnam. When she was a child, she remembers reading books and family letters about "the beautiful city of Hanoi, the culture, the wonderful dishes, and the 36 streets of the city. But when I went there, I found the streets and the food to be not as good as I had expected. The houses were run down, and the city was caught in the craze for tourist dollars. Culture? What culture? Mopeds, greed, lack of friendliness, grabbing immediately what one can, enormous poverty, and corruption. The people are not friendly. They are aggressive for dollars. Their only interest is in overcharging foreigners. They snarl at you if you question their high prices. One of our group bought a grapefruit; when she turned it over, it was rotten. The seller refused to take it back."

Chi spoke of the poverty which she and her family experienced in Vietnam after 1975, when they felt fortunate if they had a little bread, and considered life good when they had a little rice to eat. She recalls also the poverty they experienced when they began their life in America. "We escaped. We started with nothing. Now we have a comfortable house and good jobs. To see poverty and hunger continuing in Vietnam is disappointing. The problem is that Vietnam has a very negative atmosphere. People here are paranoid. They fear that others are watching them and will prevent them from doing things. When I came here, I had in mind the possibility of devoting some part of my life to working in Vietnam and contributing something to my homeland. But after one week in Hanoi, I was ready to go home. So was my mother. She planned to remain for three months. After one week in Hanoi, she couldn't stand it, staying with relatives, seeing them struggle, seeing a broken down Hanoi, not the beautiful city of her youth. She changed her ticket and left soon after. All of us were deeply disappointed and do not expect to return again."

When she was in Vietnam, Chi stayed with her mother's relatives. Despite the guilt she felt at seeing how they struggled, spending time with her relatives was the one thing that she cherished. "They are able to survive; somehow they find a way. I liked the family ties and cooperation. Despite everything, this has been maintained better in Vietnam than in the U.S.A. We're losing that in America. In Vietnam you see children in a family helping out, such as working in a family restaurant. That's good. But other than that, I sense an overwhelming negativity here. In America, you see a sense of opportunity and growth; if you work hard, you can achieve. But in Vietnam, people seem to be held back. They have no sense of direction except for taking advantage of immediate profit for the moment without thought of tomorrow. Get the buck today. Forget tomorrow. And everywhere, you are stopped by petty corruption and harassment. It's very discouraging."

Chi described several instances of harassment. "When we came into Hanoi, the immigration official refused to accept a properly prepared visa of one of our party. He said that person must fill out a new form. Someone in line muttered, 'Give him five dollars.' Another person in our party did that and passed right through without filling out extra forms. This kind of harassment is to pull money from people. The police do that too. They arbitrarily stopped a minibus that we had rented and required payments 'for coffee money.' In Hanoi, this happened quite a few times. I don't like it at all."

But her worst experience was with the police. "When we had to register with the police for staying with our relatives, they asked me questions for hours. 'When did you leave the country? Why are you coming back?' At first they said we came too late to complete the forms because we had come only one half hour before closing. Then they asked me questions until nearly midnight. At 11:50, I said that my mother wanted me home before midnight. Since I am a young woman, they accepted that. Otherwise, who knows how long they would have kept me there?"

Chi grew up in Saigon. The house where she spent her childhood was confiscated, and she had mixed feelings about going to see it again. "It is painful to think of seeing my childhood house again. I had a good childhood, and now to see the house will make me sad. But I will go to see it. I think Vietnam has changed from what I remember. Or maybe it is I who have changed. Maybe Vietnam is the same, but after living in America, coming up from being a refugee with nothing to a life that is comfortable, though not easy, I have a different perspective on what I see in Vietnam."

ACHIEVEMENTS: VIETNAMESE AMERICAN IMPACTS

Vietnamese refugees and immigrants have benefited in many ways from coming to the United States. For those who are refugees, the United States has been a place of protection from war, persecution, and hunger. For both refugees and immigrants, it has been a place where many have discovered new freedoms and opportunities. Many have been able to take advantage of educational and employment opportunities that would not have been available to them in their homeland. And many have acquired a level of material prosperity, a standard of living, and a physical comfort in living arrangements that previously they had not known. Increasing numbers of younger people have come to embrace attitudes and behaviors related to individualism that were unknown or unacceptable in their homeland. And when they return to visit the land of their ancestors, they often find that they are far more American and far less Vietnamese than they had previously realized.

This is not to say that all Vietnamese immigrants, refugees, and their American-born descendants have benefited significantly, that what America offers has come to them without a cost, or that all are happy in the United States. As we have seen, just over one quarter of the Vietnamese in America live under the poverty line. These people typically live in violent inner-city areas plagued with gangs, deteriorating schools, unemployment, and conflicts between themselves and other ethnic groups. Whatever their income level, there are growing divisions between the elderly who yearn for a traditional way of life that is gone, and younger Vietnamese who have bought into the American dream, even if it is not always attainable.

For better or worse, whether other Americans now want them here or not, and whether or not they themselves are happy or unhappy at being here, the Vietnamese are here to stay. They are a part of America and have contributed to this country in important ways. In places where they have clustered in large numbers, they have revitalized deteriorating sections of towns and cities. Often they have taken jobs other Americans avoid or reject. In many industries, the Vietnamese have gained a reputation for efficiency, hard work, and high standards of performance. The median incomes of Vietnamese Americans exceed the national median income. And as we have seen, most of the recipients of assistance are the new arrivals; the Vietnamese typically become economically self-sufficient within five years or less. In school, many have excelled and literally set new standards of achievement. Many have gone into the sciences and the professions, and one Vietnamese, Dr. Eugene Trinh, has circled the earth as an astronaut. In culture, the Vietnamese of America have brought rich traditions of music, poetic recitation, art, stunning crafts, and other aesthetic activities, often blending Western and Asian elements. In cuisine, delicious new dishes and foods have been introduced to America. In politics, the number of Vietnamese who have become citizens and who are registered voters has climbed. In recent years, a Vietnamese has become a councilman in the city of Westminster, California, others have run for Congress and for the San Francisco Board of Supervisors; and still others are actively involved in local as well as wider political issues. A particularly significant development is the rise of voluntary organizations, often run by students and young professionals, that provide services, not only for the Vietnamese, but for others in the community as well.

The Vietnamese do face problems, such as the rising power of gangs, and the continuing poverty of pockets of some Vietnamese Americans, typically the elderly and those with major health problems. But these problems are not unique to the Vietnamese; they are characteristic of poverty anywhere in America. Furthermore, the trend seems clear: as each year passes, the economic strength of the Vietnamese community grows.

Although the Vietnamese are rightly proud of the spectacular economic and educational successes of some of their people, especially those of the first wave who have been here the longest, my sense is that these high visibility achievements are not the primary measure of success in their own terms. Many Vietnamese have experienced traumatic disruption of their families or their own lives, through war, persecution by the Communists, refugee flight, or detention in refugee camps, sometimes for years on end. Success for these people is the resumption of some measure of normality in their lives. Having a place to stay, having children attend school (rare in Vietnam until recently), having a chance at employment (also rare and often specifically denied them in Vietnam), all these are normal, good, and an important measure of success, for they indicate the stabilization of their previously fractured lives. By the same token, family conflict and the drifting apart of family members constitutes failure, even if all adults are well educated professionals or are otherwise successfully employed. That is one reason why both old and young, though they often disagree, regret family schisms.

BEYOND THE SECOND DECADE

As Vietnamese Americans enter their third decade as a significant ethnic group in America, two issues are of increased concern among them. For one, many Vietnamese are deeply worried about the loosening of family ties. Older people, in particular, consider the family as they knew it to be disintegrating. Certainly it is changing. Elders, especially those who have had difficulty learning and speaking English, feel devastated by these changes. They feel lonely and isolated, and some wish to return to the land of their birth. The second issue is cultural. Again, older people fear that their cultural heritage is becoming lost in America. They are dismayed at the declining level of competence in the use of their native language by younger people, and the loss of customs and social etiquette.

Both of these concerns are open to differing interpretations. As studies by Kibria and others have shown, the family is not necessarily deteriorating. It is changing, but in ways that are neither stereotypically traditional nor American. This could be interpreted, not as disintegration, but transformation. Similarly, the fear of cultural loss may be viewed in different ways, especially in areas where there are large pockets of Vietnamese. The Vietnamese have a varied cultural life. Pre-1975 songs in the style of what is called the New or Golden or Before the War Music are still popular with many older Vietnamese in the United States. This style uses Vietnamese music, Western instrumentation, and Vietnamese lyrics, and also borrows some tunes from folk and traditional music. In the United States, the premier composer is Pham Duy. Pham Dinh Chuong, recently deceased, was a highly regarded composer and performer. Others include Duc Huy and Anh Viet.

There are some attempts to bridge Vietnamese and American cultures. For example, in Minneapolis, Cung Tien has integrated Western and Vietnamese music, organizing a concert with Vietamese singers accompanied by American musicians. Several young musicians in Houston and Los Angeles have been trained in American music schools. In southern California, the Vietnamese American Arts and Letters Association, founded in 1991, has begun to sponsor art exhibits, literary discussions, concerts, and other events to draw both Vietnamese and American writers and artists. Some musicians and singers are equally at home with Western classical and Vietnamese music, and concerts featuring both traditions are occurring, though the audiences are generally small. Throughout the United States, Vietnamese artists draw on Western and Asian traditions. For example, the painter Huong has been influenced by Picasso but utilizes Vietnamese themes, a practice followed by several artists. Her works have been shown in galleries throughout the United States and in several other countries. And Vietnamese are turning up in sports as well as in mainstream media such as television and films.

The area where I live, Santa Clara County in the Santa Clara Valley of Northern California, also reveals a lively Vietnamese cultural life, some of which aims to preserve traditions, but others which expand on them. Ceremonies include two New Year celebrations, as well as celebrations for the mythical emperor Hung Vuong, the Trung sisters who revolted against the Chinese, and several others.

As in Southern California, there is a great deal of musical activity in Santa Clara County. There have been some memorable concerts as well as art exhibitions. Within a period of ten days in August, 1995, four Vietnamese performances took place: a *Before the War Music* concert in memory of Pham Dinh Chuong, which filled an auditorium with about one thousand people; a four hour concert of popular music in the local baseball stadium, featuring 20 musicians and performers and drawing about 8000 fans; a Contemporary Viet Night, featuring dancer Maura Nguyen Donohue, and Club O' Noodles, a young, socially conscious comedy, music, and dance group; and finally a performance by composer and singer Son Van Trinh, who combines Vietnamese folk, blues, jazz, rock, and classical into his Vietnamese contemporary pop music.

Video music tapes are extremely popular among the Vietnamese, as are Chinese Kung Fu movies dubbed into Vietnamese. Music tapes cut across the generations of old and young, as younger singers perform some of the older music. More recent popular Western music is attracting the younger Vietnamese in America, who creatively blend it with some Vietnamese genres. These younger performers in turn are influencing music in Vietnam. As Professor Phong T. Nguyen observes, Vietnamese musicians in America perform a wide variety of genres: "folk songs, chamber music, theater, Buddhist chant, Caodaist chant, Hoahaoist chant, temple ritual chant, possession chant, the Catholic mass, popular songs, and Western dance." In addition, Western and Vietnamese musicians are collaborating in musical performances. He concludes, "Though music of the Vietnamese immigrants still sounds exotic to American ears, it is now part of the multicultural American society" (Phong T. Nguyen 1994: 47-51, photos pp. 48, 51).

Professors James Lull and Roger Wallis describe a type of Vietnamese *New Wave* music which is "uptempo, insistently dance-oriented music that reflects the energy and optimism of its youthful fans." It also is an expression of their distinctive, culturally diverse identities. "New wave fashions—black and white colors, silky textures, loose fitting pleated slacks, short skirts and high heels, padded shoulders on the suit jackets, high-buttoned shirts, polka dots on the accessories, the black hair moussed straight up in front—quickly distinguish the Vietnamese, especially in San Jose, a city where styling out for other residents usually means changing jeans....The Vietnamese use selected elements from the international music industry to create new sounds that help form and support their own cultural identities." Lull and Wallis see this new popular scene as primarily imitative: "They are content to copy songs well, to imitate Madonna's look, and to perform the lambada gracefully, rather than invent new styles of sound and movement" (Lull and Wallis 1992: 216-217; 231,232).

But even imitation can be creative. In her study of Karaoke among Vietnamese Americans, Deborah Wong notes, "Karaoke is one of many examples of how people reclaim the mass media and make it their own again" (Wong 1994: 163). A case in point is Miss That Thao, who has performed as a professional singer, and has elaborate Karaoke equipment in her home. She sang for me in Vietnamese, French, and English. Deborah Wong's remarks about Karaoke in a Southern California restaurant apply to what I heard in Thao's home: "When Vietnamese Americans sing karaoke tunes...they freely range between possible selves: for a few moments, they can be transported back to a Vietnam that no longer exists, or they can project themselves into uniquely immigrant images of the California dream. Either way, it seems to me, these videos and laserdiscs are a means by which Vietnamese Americans create a moment, however fleeting, and insert themselves into it ."(Wong 1994:164).

Santa Clara County is home to a number of writers who write both in Vietnamese and English, and we are now seeing bilingual prose and poetry books. There are several high school literary magazines, and occasional college publications that feature a wide range of subjects both in Vietnamese and in English. Vietnamese nightclubs feature dancing, while numerous coffee shops and dozens of Vietnamese restaurants cater to a wide clientele. The best bakeries and pastry shops in Santa Clara County are Vietnamese, many of whose chefs have been trained in Paris. As in Southern California's

Little Saigon, there are numerous Vietnamese newspapers, magazines, radio shows, and television programs. There are Vietnamese language classes for children at many of the Buddhist pagodas and Christian churches of the Valley. And for adults, there are college and university level academic courses of study in the Vietnamese language, culture, history, and literature.

The significance of these cultural developments for the Santa Clara Valley where I live is considerable. Vietnamese cultural traditions are neither fading away, nor are they removed from American cultural life. The Vietnamese are interacting with Americans, contributing to the cultural development of the valley. Of the 24,000 students who attend the university where I teach, 6,000 are Vietnamese; this also is not an insignificant impact.

True, the Vietnamese cultural elements I describe are not what one would have seen in the Vietnam of the 1960s or early 1970s. Hardly ever does one now hear traditional poetic singing recitation, and many youngsters have never heard it. But then again, the cultural elements of those years were not quite the same as those of the 1870s, or the 1770s. Cultures change, and they always have. That they have changed does not mean that they have disintegrated; as with the family, these traditions, at least in the short run, might be transforming.

However, we should not forget that for the Vietnamese elders who reside in America, the cultural losses they describe are real and deep. They signify the passing of a way of life, much of which has not been transmitted to their children, and even less to their grandchildren: etiquette, subtleties of behavior and language, rural work songs, older styles of poetry and music, a special bond between family members, various ritual traditions, and a precious sense of identity that is shared less and less by the young. American scholars, focusing on paths to educational and economic success, may say that younger Vietnamese are not Americanizing wholeheartedly, but for many older Vietnamese, who are looking at social and cultural losses, these younger people are becoming American in crucial ways. Young Vietnamese do not feel a tie to the old traditions as do their parents; they are more comfortable being American.

Colonel Tran Dinh Bui sums up the concerns of many elders, "Great changes have occurred in Vietnam over the past one hundred years, but there the Vietnamese were the majority in their homeland. Here in America, we are a minority that will be absorbed. The first two generations of Vietnamese in America will maintain Vietnamese traditions; the generation of my grandchildren will not. What we will see is not disintegration, not transformation, but Americanization. They will follow the patterns taken by many other ethnic minorities in America; they will become one flower in the garden."

Dr. Alexander Hao Nguyen, 27, has a different view; his conception of being Vietnamese does not rest on maintaining all of the old ways. He sees no contradiction in being mainstream American in the office and Vietnamese at home. His identity is situational; it shifts according to circumstance. Dr. Nguyen says he has retained the core values and traditions of the Vietnamese, and he believes that the next generation of Vietnamese will also retain them. One thing is certain: Vietnamese traditions in America are changing. I hope that what replaces them will become as meaningful and central to the younger generation of Vietnamese in America as the older traditions were for their elders.

References

Anonymous.
 1990. "1975: The Vietnam I Never Knew." First part of "Vietnamese Refugees: The Three Perspectives." *Across the Sea.* University of California, Berkeley, California: Vietnamese American Student Publications. No. 1, September-October. p. 7.

Antypa, Urania.
 1994. "Cham Nationals Overseas." *Proceedings of the Seminar on Champa.* Rancho Cordova, CA: Southeast Asia Community Resource Center, pp. 111-120.

Aurora Foundation.
 1989. *Violations of Human Rights in the Socialist Republic of Vietnam: April 1975-December 1988.* Atherton, California: Aurora Foundation.

Baer, Florence E.
 1982. "'Give me...your huddled masses': Anti-Vietnamese Refugee Lore and the 'Image of Limited Good.'" *Western Folklore.* October: pp. 275-291.

Bao Ninh.
 1993. *The Sorrow Of War: A Novel.* London: Martin Secker & Warburg. U.S.A. ed. 1995: New York: Pantheon [translation of *Noi Buon Chien Tranh.* 1991. Ha Noi: Nha Xuat Ban Hoi Nha Van (Writer's Association Publishing House)].

Benson, Janet.
 1994. "The Effects of Packinghouse Work on Southeast Asian Refugee families." in *Newcomers in the Workplace: Immigrants and the Restructuring of the U.S. Economy.* editors Louise Lamphere, Alex Stepick, and Guillermo Grenier. Philadelphia: Temple University Press, pp. 99-126.

Butler, David.
 1985. *The Fall of Saigon.* New York: Simon and Schuster.

Buttinger, Joseph.
 1972. *Vietnam: A Dragon Defiant.* New York: Praeger Publishers, Inc.

134 • REFERENCES

California Department of Finance.
1994. *Estimates of Refugees in California Counties and the State: 1991 and 1992.* Report SR 91-92. March. Demographic Research Unit.

Camino, Linda, and Ruth Krulfeld, eds.
1994. *Reconstructing Lives, Recapturing Meaning: Refugee Identity, Gender, and Culture Change.* Basel, Switzerland: Gordon and Breach.

Caplan, Nathan, John K. Whitmore, and Marcella H. Choy.
1989. *The Boat People and Achievement in America. A Study of Family Life, Hard Work, and Cultural Values.* Ann Arbor: University of Michigan Press.

Caplan, Nathan, Marcella H. Choy, and John K. Whitmore.
1991. *Children of the Boat People. A Study of Educational Success.* Ann Arbor: University of Michigan Press.

Cluck, Eunice.
1994. *The Vietnamese Community in Orange County.* Report prepared for United Way of Orange County. pp. 195-208.

Dang Nguyen Anh.
1991. "The Position of Women in Two Rural Communes." in *Sociological Studies on the Vietnamese Family.* edited by Rita Liljestrom and Tuong Lai. Hanoi: Social Sciences Publishing House, pp. 187-196.

Das, K.
1978. "The Tragedy of the KG 0729: *Far Eastern Economic Review.* Vol. 101, No. 45, December 22, p. 13.

Das, K. and Guy Sacerdoti.
1978. "Economics of a human cargo;" "Digging in for a long stay." *Far Eastern Economic Review.* Vol. 101, No. 45, December 22, pp. 10-12.

Department of Social Services, State of California.
1993. *Annual Recipient Report on AFDC, Social Services, Nonassistance Food Stamps, Gain, and RCA Ethnic Origin and Primary Language.* April. Sacramento, California: Statistical Services.

Do Anh.
1992. "Abandoned Again." *Orange County Register.* June 9, pp. 1-2.

Do Thai Dong.
1991. "Modifications of the Traditional Family in the South of Vietnam." in *Sociological Studies on the Vietnamese Family.* edited by Rita Liljestrom and Tuong Lai. Hanoi: Social Sciences Publishing House, pp. 79-96.

Duiker, William J.
1995a. *Vietnam: Nation in Revolution.* Second Edition. Boulder, Colorado: Westview Press.

_____.
1995b. *The Sacred War: Nationalism and Revolution in a Divided Nation.* New York: McGraw Hill.

Ebihara, May, Carol A. Mortland, and Judy Ledgerwood, eds.
   1994. *Cambodian Culture since 1975: Homeland and Exile.* Ithaca, New
      York: Cornell University Press.

Engelmann, Larry.
   1995. "Making Room for 140,000 Refugees." *San Jose Mercury News.*
      June 25. pp. 1, 4-5C.

Epstein, Aaron.
   1995. "Justices to rule on census dispute." *San Jose Mercury News.* Sep-
      tember 28. p. 6A

Felsman, J.Kirk, Mark C. Johnson, Frederick T.L. Leong, and Irene C.
Felsman.
   1989. *Vietnamese Amerasians: Practical Implications of Current Research.*
      Washington, D.C.: Office of Refugee Resettlement, Family Sup-
      port Administration, Department of Health and Human Servic-
      es. December.

Finnan, Christine Robinson.
   1981. "Occupational Assimilation of Refugees." *International Migra-
      tion Review.* Vol. 15, No. 1, Spring. pp. 292-309.

Fisher, Gail.
   1992. "Coming Home." *Los Angeles Times.* Section BB Orange County,
      Part Two. Thursday, November 26, pp. BB1, 6-7.

Freeman, James M.
   1989. *Hearts of Sorrow: Vietnamese American Lives.* Stanford, California:
      Stanford University Press.

Freeman, James M. and Nguyen Dinh Huu.
   1991. Film Review of How to Behave. *Journal of Asian Studies.* Vol. 50,
      No. 2, May: pp. 479-481.

_____.
   in press. "Terror at Dong Rek." *Global Justice.*

_____.
   n.d.   *Voices from the Camps: The Abuse and Neglect of Children Seeking
      Asylum.* in preparation.

Freeman, James M., Huu Nguyen, and Peggy Hartsell.
   1985. "The Tribal Lao Training Project." *Cultural Survival Quarterly.*
      Vol. 9, No. 2, pp. 10-12.

Gold, Steven J.
   1992. *Refugee Communities: A Comparative Field Study.* Newbury Park,
      California: Sage Publications.

Gourevitch, Philip
   1994: "Vietnam: The Bitter Truth," Review of South Wind Changing
      by Jade Ngoc Quang Huynh. *New York Review of Books.* Decem-
      ber 22, pp. 55-58.

Grant, Bruce and 'Age' Contributors.
   1979. *The Boat People: An 'Age' Investigation*. Harmondsworth, Middlesex, England: Penguin Books.

Haines, David W., ed.
   1985. *Refugees in the United States: A Reference Handbook*. Westport, Connecticut: Greenwood Press.

Hein, Jeremy.
   1993. *States and International Migrants: The Incorporation of Indochinese Refugees in the United States and France*. Boulder, Colorado: Westview Press.

Henkin, Alan B. and Nguyen, Liem Thanh.
   1981. *Between Two Cultures: The Vietnamese in America*. Saratoga, California: R and E. Publishers.

Hickey, Gerald Cannon.
   1982a. *Sons of the Mountains: Ethnohistory of the Vietnamese Central Highlands to 1954*. New Haven: Yale University Press.

_____.
   1982b. *Fire in the Forest: Ethnohistory of the Vietnamese Central Highlands, 1954-1976*. New Haven: Yale University Press.

Huynh, Jade Ngoc Quang.
   1994. *South Wind Changing*. Saint Paul, Minnesota: Graywolf Press.

Huynh, Minh.
   1995. "Plant Care and Americanization: A Personal View." *Suvannabhumi*. Newsletter of the Program for Southeast Asian Studies at Arizona State University, Tempe, Arizona. Vol. 6, No. 2, May. pp. 7-8.

Indochina Interchange.
   1995. "War Statistics Released." Vol. 5, No. 1, p. 29. June.

Isaacs, Arnold R.
   1983 (1984). *Without Honor: Defeat in Vietnam and Cambodia*. New York: Vintage.

Karnow, Stanley.
   1983 (revised edition 1991). *Vietnam: A History*. New York: Viking Press.

_____.
   1993. "In Orange County's Little Saigon, Vietnamese try to bridge two worlds." *Smithsonian*. pp. 28-39.

Kelly, Gail Paradise.
   1977. *From Vietnam to America*. Boulder, Colorado: Westview Press.

Kennedy, Edward M.
   1981. "Refugee Act of 1980." *International Migration Review*. Vol. 15, No. 1, Spring, p. 141-156.

Khuat Thu Hong.
1991. "Overview of Sociological Research on Family in Vietnam." in *Sociological Studies on the Vietnamese Family*. edited by Rita Liljestrom and Tuong Lai. Hanoi: Social Sciences Publishing House, pp. 197-214.

Kibria, Nazli.
1993. *Family Tightrope: The Changing Lives of Vietnamese Americans.* Princeton, New Jersey: Princeton University Press.

Jamieson, Neil L.
1993. *Understanding Vietnam.* Berkeley and Los Angeles, California: University of California Press.

Le Ngoan.
1994. *Profile of the Vietnamese American Community.* Preliminary Draft. National Congress of Vietnamese in America. (No address).

Le Thuan.
1994. "Regards to the Past. North Vietnam Journey Brings Honor to Ancestors and Hopes for the Future." *Los Angeles Times.* Section E. Lifestyle. Wednesday, September 28. pp. E-1, 8-9.

Lee, Mary.
1979. "Long wait for the promised land." *Far Eastern Economic Review.* Vol. 106, No. 45, p. 30.

Liljestrom, Rita and Tuong Lai, editors.
1991. *Sociological Studies on the Vietnamese Family.* Hanoi: Social Sciences Publishing House.

Liu, William T., Maryanne Mamanna, and Alice Murata.
1979. *Transition to Nowhere: Vietnamese Refugees in America.* Nashville, Tennessee: Charter House Publishers, Inc.

Marr, David G.
1971. *Vietnamese Anticolonialism 1885-1925.* Berkeley and Los Angeles, California:University of California Press.

_____.
1981. *Vietnamese Tradition on Trial 1920-1945.* Berkeley and Los Angeles, California: University of California Press.

Loescher, Gil and John A. Scanlon.
1986. *Calculated Kindness: Refugees and America's Half-Open Door, 1945-Present.* New York: Free Press.

Lull, James and Roger Wallis.
1992. "The Beat of West Vietnam." in *Popular Music and Communication.* edited by James Lull. Newbury Park, California: Sage Publications, pp. 207-236.

Luong, Hy V.
1992. *Revolution in the Village. Tradition and Transformation in North Vietnam, 1925-1988.* Honolulu: University of Hawaii Press.

Ministry of Labor, War Invalids, and Social Affairs.
1995. In *Vietnam News Agency*. Statistics on Vietnam War Deaths. April 3. See also Indochina Interchange.

Montero, Darrel.
1979. *Vietnamese Americans: Patterns of Resettlement and Socioeconomic Adaptation in the United States*. Boulder, Colorado: Westview Press.

Muntarbhorn, Vitit.
1992. *The Status of Refugees in Asia*. Oxford and New York: Oxford University Press.

Myo Thant and Richard W.A. Vokes.
1993. "Vietnam and ASEAN: Near-Term Prospects of Economic Co-operation." in *Vietnam's Dilemmas and Options*, edited by Mya Than and Joseph L.H. Tan. Singapore: ASEAN Economic Research Unit, Institute of Southeast Asian Studies, pp. 237-258.

Ngo Vinh Long.
1991 (1973). *Before the Revolution: The Vietnamese Peasants Under the French*. New York: Columbia University Press.

Nguyen Long with Harry H. Kendall.
1981. *After Saigon Fell: Daily Life Under the Vietnamese Communists*. University of California, Berkeley: Institute of East Asian Studies.

Nguyen Manh Hung.
1985. "Vietnamese." in *Refugees in the United States: A Reference Handbook*, ed. by David W. Haines, Westport, Connecticut: Greenwood Press., pp. 195-208.

Nguyen, Phong T.
1994. "Transplanting Vietnamese Music to the United States." *The Ky 21 (The 21st Century)*. No. 66, October, pp. 47-51.

Nguyen Tu Chi.
1991. "Preliminary Notes on the Family of the Viet." in *Sociological Studies on the Vietnamese Family*. edited by Rita Liljestrom and Tuong Lai. Hanoi: Sciences Publishing House, pp. 65-77.

Nhat Tien, Duong Phuc, Vu Thanh Thuy.
1981. *Pirates on the Gulf of Siam*. Report from the Vietamese Boat People Living in the Refugee Camp in Songkhla-Thailand. San Diego, California: Boat People S.O.S. Committee.

Pham Van Son, editor.
1968. *The Viet Cong Tet Offensive*. Saigon: Republic of Vietnam Armed Forces.

Pike, Douglas.
1966. *The Viet Cong*. Cambridge, MA: M.I.T. Press.

Portes, Alejandro and Ruben G. Rumbaut.
1990. *Immigrant America: A Portrait*. Berkeley and Los Angeles: University of California Press.

Ranard, Donald A. and Douglas F. Gilzow.
   1989. "The Amerasians." *In America: Perspectives on Refugee Resettlement*. Washington, D.C. Refugee Service Center, Center for Applied Linguistics, Number 4, June.

Reimers, David M.
   1992. *Still the Golden Door: The Third World Comes to America*. New York: Columbia University Press. 2nd edition.

Richardson, Michael.
   1979. "How many died?" *Far Eastern Economic Review*. Vol. 106, No. 43, October 26, p. 34.

Rieff, David.
   1990. "The Transformation of America." Review of Hearts of Sorrow by James M. Freeman. *Times Literary Supplement*. May 25-31, pp. 543-544.

Rumbaut, Ruben.
   1995. "Vietnamese, Laotian, and Cambodian Americans." in *Asian Americans: Contemporary Issues and Trends*. ed. by Pyong Gap Min. Thousand Oaks, California: Sage Publications, pp. 232-270.

Rumbaut, Ruben and Kenji Ima.
   1988. *The Adaptation of Southeast Asian Refugee Youth: A Comparative Study*. Washington D.C. U.S. Office of Refugee Resettlement.

Rutledge, Paul James.
   1992. *The Vietnamese Experience in America*. Bloomington and Indianapolis: University of Indiana Press.

Snepp, Frank.
   1978. *Decent Interval. An Insider's Account of Saigon's Indecent End Told by the CIA's Chief Strategy Analyst in Vietnam*. New York: Vintage.

Socialist Republic of Vietnam.
   1992. *National Report on Two Years' Implementation of the United Nations Convention on the Rights of the Child*. Hanoi: Committee for the Protection and Care of Children.

Starr, Paul D.
   1981. "Troubled Waters: Vietnamese Fisherfolk on America's Gulf Coast." *International Migration Review*. Vol. 15, No. 1, Spring: pp. 226-238.

Stein, Barry.
   1979. "Occupational Adjustment of Refugees: The Vietnamese in the United States." *International Migration Review*. Vol 13, No. 1. Spring: pp. 25-45.

Swearington, Roger and Hammond Rolph.
   1967. *Communism in Vietnam*. Chicago: American Bar Association.

Taylor, Keith.
1983. *The Birth of Vietnam.*Berkeley and Los Angeles: University of California Press.

Tran De.
1995. "Reunion at Tent City." *San Jose Mercury News.* June 25, pp. 1, 24A

Tran, Qui-Phiet.
1993: "Exile and Home in Contemporary Vietnamese American Feminine Writing." *Amerasia Journal.* Volume 19, Number 3, 71-83.

_____.
1995. "Exiles in the Land of the Free: Vietnamese Artists and Writers in America, 1975 to the Present." *The Ky 21 (21st Century).* Number 73, May, 45-49.

United States Catholic Conference, Marilyn Lacey.
1985. *In Our Father's Land: Vietnamese Amerasians in the United States.*Washington, D.C.: United States Catholic Conference.

U.S. Department of Commerce, Economics and Statistics Administration, Bureau of the Census.
1990a. Census of Population. *General Population Characteristics, United States.*1990 CP1-1.

_____.
1990b. *Asians and Pacific Islanders in the United States.*1990 CP3-5.

_____.
1990c. *The Foreign-Born Population in the United States.* 1990 CP3-1.

_____.
1990d. *General Population Characteristics, California.* 1990 CP-1-6. Section 1 of 3.

_____.
1990e. *Social and Economic Characteristics, California.* 1990 CP-2-6. Section 1 of 4.

1990 Census, Santa Clara County, California.
1990 Census of Population and Housing. California State Census Data Center. Race Group: Vietnamese; State: California; County: Santa Clara. PB16-PB18.

U.S. Department of State.
Southeast Asian Refugee Arrivals in the U.S. and Other Countries.

Wain, Barry.
1981. *The Refused: The Agony of the Indochinese Refugees.*New York: Simon and Schuster.

Weintraub, Peter.
1978. "The exodus and the agony." *Far Eastern Economic Review.* Vol. 102, No. 51, pp. 8-11.

Weiss, Lowell.
1994. "Timing is Everything." *Atlantic Monthly*. January. pp. 32, 34-36, 44.

Welaratna, Usha.
1993. *Beyond the Killing Fields: Voices of Nine Cambodian Survivors in America*. Stanford, California: Stanford University Press.

Whitmore, John K.
1985. "Chinese from Southeast Asia." in *Refugees in the United States*. ed. by David W. Haines. Greenwood Press. Westport, Connecticut. pp. 59-76.

Wong, Deborah.
1994. "'I Want the Microphone': Mass Meditation and Agency in Asian-American Popular Music ."*The Drama Review*, 38.3 (T143), Fall, pp. 152-167.

Woodside, Alexander Barton.
1988. *Vietnam and the Chinese Model. A Comparative Study of Vietnamese and Chinese Government in the First Half of the Nineteenth Century*. Cambridge, Massachusetts, Council on East Asian Studies, Harvard University, Harvard university Press.

Zhou, Min and Carl L. Bankston, III.
1994. "Social Capital and the Adaptation of the Second Generation: The Case of Vietnamese Youth in New Orleans." *International Migration Review*. Volume XXVIII, Number 4, Winter, 821-845.

Zolberg, Aristide R., Astri Suhrke, and Sergio Aguayo.
1989. *Escape f rom Violence: Conflict and the Refugee Crisis in the Developing World*. New York and Oxford: Oxford University Press.